PRAISE FOR

THE A STRATEGIC PARTNER...

Dancing with Elephants

"A leading expert in partnerships, mergers, and acquisitions, Sochan gets inside the minds of both the startup entrepreneurs and the big guys. This book is packed with practical suggestions, examples, and tactics to keep a partnership on the right track long after the ink on the contract has dried."

–Geoffrey Moore, author of *Crossing the Chasm*, *The Gorilla Game*, and *Inside the Tornado*

"For anyone trying to navigate the often-stormy waters of strategic partnerships and alliances, this book provides markers to guide you on your voyage."

–Ed Oates, Cofounder, Oracle

"Sochan provides the ultimate 'how-to' guide to creating world-class strategic partnerships. His book includes real-life advice known only to those who have seen partnership deals made from the inside."

–Jason Wolf, General Manager, Global Technology Partners, SAP

"A great, practical guide to help you through the partnership process."

–Zia Yusuf, Partner and Managing Director, The Boston Consulting Group–Silicon Valley

The Art of
STRATEGIC
PARTNERING

DANCING WITH ELEPHANTS

How to partner with industry titans
...without getting crushed

Mark Sochan

NAK
PUBLISHING
Gilroy, California

Paperback: 978-1-7323998-0-8
E-book: 978-1-7323998-1-5

NAK Publishing
Gilroy, CA 95020
info@nakpublishing.com

Ordering Information:
Special discounts are available on quantity purchases by corporations, associations, and others. For details, contact the publisher.

Cover and interior design by DianaRussellDesign.com
Author photo by Niki Britton, 111th Photography
Illustrations and cover image sourced from CartoonStock.com, andertoons.com, cartoonbank.com, and iStock.com.

Printed in the United States of America

Publisher's Cataloging-in-Publication Data:
Names: Sochan, Mark.
Title: The art of strategic partnering : dancing with elephants / Mark Sochan.
Description: First edition. | Gilroy, California : NAK Publishing, [2018] | "How to partner with industry titans ... without getting crushed." | Includes bibliographical references and index.
Identifiers: ISBN 9781732399808 (paperback) | ISBN 9781732399815 (ebook)
Subjects: LCSH: Strategic alliances (Business) | Joint ventures. | Negotiation in business. | Entrepreneurship.
Classification: LCC HD69.S8 S63 2018 (print) | LCC HD69.S8 (ebook) | DDC 658/.044–dc23

DEDICATION

To my father,
whose wisdom and support
have made all the difference

CONTENTS

ACKNOWLEDGEMENTS

The idea for *The Art of Strategic Partnering: Dancing with Elephants* started over coffee at the Starbucks in Los Gatos, California, with Kathryn Ullrich, author of *Getting to the Top: Strategies for Career Success*. When I mentioned my lifelong dream of writing a book, she marched right out to her car and brought back a signed copy of her book. That was the spark that got the fire started.

It was some weeks later, when I sat down with another author, Robert Lauridsen, who wrote *More, Better, Different,* that the flames for the fire were fanned. In a brainstorming session, we mapped out the key ideas and the approach for the book. I truly believe that getting started is half done.

Finally, the book came to life with help from Jim Dryburgh, Beth Parker, Peter Verbica, and John Swensson. I am very grateful to high-tech industry veterans Bill Lipsin, Jason Wolf, Tom Reilly, David Leiser, and my brother, Paul Sochan, who came to the rescue and helped with initial proofreading and suggestions on improving the book.

Thanks to the creative ideas of Diana Russell, I had six fantastic book covers to choose from. It was a great experience engaging everyone in my business, social, and family network to gather feedback and opinions on everyone's favorite cover. Thanks to my copyeditor, Mark Woodworth, and to Holly Brady for strategic advice.

Thank you to Niki Britton, Pat Belanger, and Julie Belanger of the 111th Photography Group for their feedback on the cover of the book and the portrait photos.

The title of the book was another source of interesting debate. Many variations of word combinations were considered and discussed. It took a few cocktails at a C100 event and a coincidental meeting with a fellow Canadian expat, Glen Elliott, to inspire the final title.

Thanks to my entire family, especially Mary Ann, Nikolai, Aleksander, and Kristof, for enduring my endless talk about "the book." They were patient and helpful with good ideas that helped keep the momentum going.

I am grateful to my mentors over the years: Jim Dryburgh, Haig Farris, and my dad, Harry Sochan. Their constant wisdom and support have made a huge difference in my career.

And a big thanks to Terry Cunningham and Greg Kerfoot, who were incredibly inspirational leaders early in my career. They were pioneers of the concept of gaining business leverage through Strategic OEM Partnerships. It was in those exciting, heady days of a fast-growing startup company that the analogy of *Dancing with Elephants* was born.

Alright, alright, you've won your bet:
You can lift me with one hand...

INTRODUCTION

"If you can learn to stand on the shoulders of giants, you can get bigger, faster."

–Isaac Newton

With the ink barely dry on the exciting new strategic partnership contract signed just three months ago, you sit in your office and stare in disbelief at a threatening "Cease and Desist" letter written by the other company's legal counsel. What went wrong, you wonder? How could so much excitement and energy generated by this "game-changing" strategic partnership take such an unfortunate turn?

The answer is simple: Getting a deal done is just the beginning. Managing a strategic partnership and executing to clearly aligned goals is like acknowledging the hidden part of an iceberg submerged beneath the surface of the ocean water.

I know because I've been there—and continue to be there. Throughout my career, I have been passionate about partnering. With over 150 deals under my belt, I continue to gain insights into what's going on at both sides of the table, leading up to and following a partnership deal.

Despite what statistics reveal in terms of the failure rate of partnerships, I've experienced how a well-thought-out and well-managed partnership can make it possible for companies, on both sides of the table, to increase sales and revenues. I have seen how large companies have been able to fill a technology gap and leapfrog ahead of their competitors. Smaller companies have been able to leverage large distribution channels to enter new markets, increase brand awareness, lower the cost of new customer acquisition, and ultimately deliver a successful financial exit to their investors.

As a consultant in strategic partnering with a business located in California's Silicon Valley, I've had the opportunity to work both with the "elephant big guys" (today's leading, huge global technology companies) as well as with what I define as "smaller" companies and startups.

I've sat across the table with top industry executives, including Sun's Scott McNealy, Microsoft's Bob Muglia, and SAP's Chief Executive Officer, Bill McDermott. I've negotiated deals with Microsoft, Oracle, Cisco, IBM, VMware, SAP, and BMC. When advising smaller companies and startups in the United States and Canada, I've led aggressive business development and partnership strategies (and been an investor). At Partnerpedia, for example, I earned multimillion-dollar payouts for investors as a result of the company's partnership strategy and activity that I drove. As Vice President at SAP, I leveraged my experience and understanding of startup companies to create a compelling vendor partner program. The work entailed launching and building the SAP Developer Network, and then creating the partner ecosystem for the SAP NetWeaver platform.

What I've learned over the years is that the dynamics are the same, whether you're a "big guy" or an entrepreneurial company with a couple of dozen employees. Understanding and managing a partnership agreement has more to do with managing the partnership like a *business*, and distinctly not like a deal. Success lies in gaining perspective into how the other side thinks—specifically, how they set their goals and define success, even how they manage contract negotiations. These all make a difference in setting up the right deal at the beginning and then establishing the overall health of the relationship going forward.

Why This Book Is for You

The goal of this book is to share with business leaders like yourself how you can succeed at the art of strategic partnerships—not only through negotiations leading up to the contract signing, but also long after the "honeymoon" is over and the partners actually "move in" together. You could be a startup or a smaller company.[1] Yet, regardless of your size, you are looking to partner with the big guys—that is, the current giants in the technology sector, such as Apple, Microsoft, Alphabet (Google), Oracle, Intel, Cisco, Facebook, IBM, Amazon, HP Inc.+HPE, and Dell. For those outside the technology industry, the lessons are the same. Having allies on your side in the form of strategic partnerships can offer innumerable benefits to your company.

What are the compelling reasons to read this book? They are to avoid costly mistakes and to increase the probability of success.

What defines you is *one or more* of the following:

- You are considering a strategic partnership and looking for a practical, honest guide on how to avoid some of the pitfalls and increase your chances of success.

- You are already aligned with at least one partner through a partnership deal and are looking for advice on areas that have presented particular challenges or roadblocks.

- You have moved past your first partnership deal and perhaps already have a few signed contracts, but going forward you want to maximize the value of your partnerships.

The book covers setting your goals (deciding why to partner and whom to partner with); business and contract negotiations; getting through the first 12 months leading up to the launch; and managing the partnership going forward. It also covers the wider topic of ecosystems, which in today's market is increasingly relevant because of the symbiotic relationship between companies, partners, and customers. The various chapters pose questions to help you think through what's required for a successful partnership and what kind of preparation is needed in order to ensure its success.

Successfully dancing with elephants involves being able to understand the different parties' perspective, and then trying to work to find common ground. These efforts apply to the big guys the same way they apply to your company. Being able to put such skills to work has helped me complete many a successful dance. Now I pass these dance steps on to you.

Mark Sochan
Spring 2018

CHAPTER 1:

WHY PARTNER

"If you think back in time, Apple and IBM were foes. Apple and Microsoft still compete, but we can partner on more things than we compete on. And that's what customers want. [Apple users] love Office, and they want it to work on Mac better than it works on Windows, and it should."

–Tim Cook, CEO, Apple

In 1984, a serial entrepreneur named Terry Cunningham set up a software company called Crystal Services. Over the next few years, he and his partner, Greg Kerfoot, created the world's first Windows-based reporting tool, which they named Crystal Reports.

The founders firmly believed in their product but they were under no illusion as to the size of their small, Vancouver, Canada-based company or the limits of its market reach. Crystal Services was part of a family-owned business in the limited Canadian market. No one—that is, *not a single person*—knew they existed. Even though there was an emerging opportunity in the growing business intelligence market crying out for reporting software such as theirs, they knew that wasn't enough to secure success. They needed a vehicle to massively distribute their fledgling tool, "Crystal Reports." If they didn't move fast enough with their technology, someone else would surely beat them to the finish line.

The opportunity opened up when Microsoft first released Visual Basic, a relatively easy-to-use programming language for writing code. Widely adopted after its initial launch by software developers and IT professionals, Visual Basic did not include any kind of report writing technology that could easily arrange database information. Crystal Services knew what it needed to do. Its founders made the strategic decision that to leap ahead—and stay ahead—they had to form strategic partnerships with OEMs (Original Equipment Manufacturers). These large, established technology vendors would provide a bigger, faster channel to the market. In doing so, they also would embed Crystal's technology into the products of large companies, which already had influential brands, well-resourced marketing departments, and massive sales teams and channels.

I joined the company in 1993 as Director of Strategic Relations. My role was to direct and grow the partnership strategy. Over the next few years, I worked to expand its initial strategic partnership with Microsoft's Visual Basic development tool to form strategic OEM partnerships with over 150 independent software vendor (ISV) partners, including IBM, SAP, and Oracle. It was tough sledding, but the strategy worked. With Crystal Reports bundled inside the Microsoft Visual Basic package, anyone who used Visual Basic instantly became a user of Crystal Reports. By that time, the company's presence already had caught the eye of a much larger company, Seagate Technology. Seagate bought Crystal Services for about $20 million in 1994 and renamed it Crystal Decisions.

Crystal Decisions gained almost instant visibility to the global market of developers buying Visual Basic. The OEM partnerships also provided an immediate channel of distribution for the next level of sales. The company developed and released a Pro version of Crystal Reports, which it now could use in order to upsell to its partners' original customers. Before long, customers around the world depended on Crystal Reports for their database reporting solutions.

By the early 2000s, Crystal Decisions was in an ideal position to be acquired for a second time at a much higher valuation. It had become one of the strongest-performing companies in the enterprise software sector at a time when its rival, the French-American Business Objects, was intent on securing a leadership position in the business intelligence market. Like most successful strategic partnerships, both sides complemented each other with product distribution channels and geographic presence.

The cash-and-stock deal agreed to in July 2008 was worth just under $840 million (U.S.). The existing shareholders of Crystal Decisions received $300 million in cash and 26.5 million shares—the very positive results of a well-executed strategic partnership strategy.

The story of Crystal Decisions is only one example of the power of strategic partnering when used to kick-start higher growth. It provides a basis for reviewing strategic partnerships in general, the goals of such a partnership, why your company might pursue this strategy, the initial questions to ask, the rewards of partnering, and the risks if you *don't* partner.

What Is Strategic Partnering?

In recent years, there has been an increase in strategic partnerships where two companies, sometimes in different industries, link capabilities to create a much higher value proposition for the ultimate end user: the customer. It is likely that your company already has various informal partners—perhaps vendors, suppliers, outsourced service providers, and so on. But when you make a decision to formalize the relationship in some way, such alliances become strategic partners.

The partnering agreement makes it possible to pool resources, gain access to specific expertise and experience, and pursue an opportunity together. Both partners share benefits and risks, make contributions of various kinds in strategic areas, and, ideally, share the potential for future opportunities.

Countless startups and smaller, entrepreneurial companies have grown to their current size and, in many instances, achieved market dominance because they learned how to effectively partner to achieve their goals.

Strategic partnerships can take various forms. Typically, they are OEM strategic partners, reselling partners, and other strategic arrangements that aim to significantly change the dynamics in the market. The general hierarchy from low value to increasingly higher value is shown below. (A more detailed description of these is provided in chapter 2, page 25.)

HIGH • OEM license agreement where one company licenses a product and rebrands it or combines it with its existing products

• Reseller agreements where one or possibly both parties agree to sell each other's product

• Lead sharing or customer referrals

LOW • Marketing alliances to co-promote brands

What Prompts a Decision to Partner?

A conversation around partnering usually starts when one or more of the following scenarios presents itself.

An entrepreneur who is truly visionary sees the need for a new kind of product long before anyone else knows that it would add value. To get the idea implemented ahead of the competition, his or her company makes the decision to leverage the resources of strategic partners. This was the case for Crystal Decisions. Partnering with larger established technology vendors that had an existing customer base to form strategic OEM partnerships was clearly the best way to move quickly into the market.

In other instances, the CEO, an investor, or a board member strongly believes in partnering, perhaps because they've already seen how it can be successful. They may feel that, given their product and the competitive environment, it's the right path to take. Sometimes there may be interest but the CEO, the senior management team, or certain board members have questions that need to be answered. Such questions include how to pursue a partnership and whether the rewards will outweigh the risks in their particular situation.

There also can be outright objections to partnering. Some business leaders view strategic partnerships as a form of weakness that threatens to slow down the business by creating dependencies. There can also be fear about what might change once the company is aligned with a "giant." A sales partnership, for example, could mean loss of control over the sales process as well as the loss of important customer feedback loops. Other leaders might be suspicious of the motives behind the interested party. In the back of a CEO's mind, he wonders why a larger company is sniffing around about his company's products or services.

To Partner or Not to Partner

The above questions and concerns are perfectly valid. A partnership may be a critical strategy for a company looking to tap into new markets, acquire more customers, and sell more products and services. Yet it can also be tricky to manage and to make work. The process for deciding whether or not strategic partnerships are the answer for your company begins with ensuring that everyone is on board with the reasons *why* your company might choose partnering as the best strategy. What do you want to gain? What problems do you want to solve? How will you measure the partnerhip's success? What's standing in your way of success?

"WHO US, PARTNER?"
HOW TO ANSWER THE QUESTION

There are different ways of looking at the question of partnering and whether a partnership strategy is the right choice for your company. It can be helpful to look at this question through the lenses of "core" and "context."

These terms were coined by the organization theorist and author Geoffrey Moore. Moore acquired a reputation as a marketing guru in the early 1990s following the publication of *Crossing the Chasm: Marketing and Selling Disruptive Products to Mainstream*, in which he focused on the technology adoption life cycle. In a later book, *Dealing with Darwin: How Great Companies Innovate at Every Phase of their Evolution*, Moore looked at what companies need to do in order to grow and continue to innovate.

Moore's framework for establishing a company's strategic importance focuses on activities that he names *core* and *context*:

CORE activities are those that increase the sustainable competitive advantage of a company as well as create value for customers in a way that is hard for competitors to replicate.

CONTEXT activities are everything else, from managing real estate to conducting HR and inventory management functions. These activities are important, but they don't differentiate you in any way. For example, context activities are often the ones that a company chooses to outsource.

Examining core and context helps an organization focus on what it does best, what it might want to build upon, and where it might invest in expertise outside the company. For many companies, partnerships make it possible to support core activities by aligning with experts in other areas, such as sales training, marketing, brand development, and the like. On the other hand, a niche-services company may be ideal for partners looking to offload what they see as context activities that are nonessential to their differentiation.

Goals of Partnering

Conducting a review of your business priorities and the benefits of partnership is essential to analyze whether your company would benefit from a partnership strategy.

The ultimate goal of any partnership strategy is to increase business value. Typically, this is accomplished by growing sales. As a business priority, this is the same whether you are the huge Google or a small San Francisco startup called Spoke. But for a small, unknown company there can be tremendous business value creation in the mere association with a larger, well-established company brand. The association with a large brand can create huge marketing leverage and market exposure that otherwise could have taken years of effort and large investments in marketing activities to establish the same level of market awareness independently.

The way in which you achieve your partnership goals, however, generally depends on the size and nature of the company. Smaller companies may be looking to increase revenue through a leveraged partnership brand and larger sales channels. Large companies typically look to a partnering strategy to speed up their innovation cycle and thereby improve their product competitiveness by adding features and capabilities to an existing product.

The decision to partner should always start with having a clear understanding of the reasons why a partnership strategy would be best for your particular company, looking at the value you might bring to a larger "giant," and then knowing how to test the waters, prepare a solid business case, and devise a plan that manages the risks and objections.

APPLE VERSUS MICROSOFT

The best example of setting priorities that determine a partnership strategy can be found in the rivalry between Microsoft and Apple. One pursued a partnering strategy, while the other chose vertical integration.

Early on, Microsoft made a strategic decision to aggressively expand through channel partners to get its DOS operating system into as many hardware brands as possible. Microsoft's strategy was very effective in capturing the market quickly. It opened up the market for third-party software developers that then created a large selection of applications for a growing number of customers.

To execute on the strategy, however, Microsoft gave up control over both the way computers "looked" and the customer experience provided by its numerous vendor partners. Sure, the design of DOS was clunky and you had to be a techie to understand it, but because everyone agreed on a standardized platform the hardware cost was lower and the availability of third-party applications was greater, Microsoft soon dominated the market. As a result, it won the first "battle of the operating system wars," hands down.

Apple, by contrast, took a very different approach. Its cofounder, Steve Jobs, deliberately chose a vertical integration strategy in order to control the design aesthetics and overall customer experience. Apple had its own box, its own chip (until 1972), and its own operating system and applications—the whole thing was theirs. Because of Apple's strategic priorities, it did not make sense for the company to create OEM partnerships like Microsoft did.

For years, both companies stayed true to their overall priorities. Microsoft won the operating system wars, while Apple, with less than 10 percent of the global market, stayed true to its commitment to design aesthetics and good customer experience.

Epilogue: Over time, Apple adjusted its strategic priorities, and as a result, the company opened itself up to outside partnerships. When Jobs returned to lead the ailing company in 1997, Apple phased out its own PowerPC chips and, through a partnership with Intel begun in 2006, started putting Intel processors inside Macs. You will read in chapter 7 how Apple won the mobile app wars by embracing external application developer partnerships (though with strict quality and consistency controls). Google took the Microsoft approach of an open mobile operating system, called "Android," that allowed a proliferation of various hardware and apps. The completely open approach once again became known for clunky design and less-reliable apps, while Apple maintained a more consistent, user-friendly interface and dependable apps.

Benefits of Partnering

For the smaller company, the benefits of partnering fall into one or more of the following categories:

- Marketing resources

- Sales reach

- Brand leverage

These categories overlap and, in most instances, the impact is felt across all three areas.

This certainly was the case for Crystal Decisions. Its strategic partnership through a bundling agreement with Microsoft leveraged a combination of the following benefits, making it possible to quickly grab both market and mindshare for reporting software.

Marketing: Large companies employ hundreds of people who work in marketing and communications across multiple business units, and they have ample resources for market research and development. A smaller company may not even have a dedicated marketing department. A partnership provides access to such marketing teams, and to their deep knowledge of their industry and market. With expertise in segmentation, targeting, competitive intelligence, and positioning, corporate marketing teams know, for example, how to estimate the time required for a product release, or how to determine the right product strategy when entering a new market.

At trade shows and conferences, larger companies have serious clout attracting attention and audience traffic. When a partner's name or logo is displayed in a booth or on a sign or in a presentation, it can be viewed by hundreds of potential customers. When communication departments issue press releases about new partnerships and products, the message about your product reaches a global audience, giving credibility to your brand. All these benefits combine to complement sales activity and brand development.

Sales Channels: A smaller company will most likely have a limited number of sales personnel. Even if you decide to grow your own sales force, it takes time to train them, develop a pipeline of potential sales leads, tune things up, try different approaches, create a solid value proposition, and finally monitor success.

Acquiring new customers is difficult, time-consuming, and resource intensive. Research shows that it costs five times as much to attract a new customer as it does to keep an existing one. In addition, the probability of selling to an existing customer is 60 to 70 percent, while the probability of selling to a new prospect is 5 to 20 percent.[2]

Most innovative companies feel pressured to get a product out in a compressed time frame. But, in a smaller company, it takes time to move through any sales cycle, particularly if its product and brand are not well known. There's also a cost for any sales cycle. Without the resources to move quickly into the market, there is a greater likelihood that a competitor might release a similar or more innovative product.

Partnering with a larger company can change all of this. Leveraging the trusted relationships between the partner's sales force and its customer base can significantly accelerate the sales cycle for your product. It is now possible to tap into the existing customer base of a larger company, which could be a gold mine of hundreds or even thousands of loyal customers.

All of this actually gives you a tremendous advantage. Partnering gives you access to sales resources that provide exposure to your product and brand that would be challenging to achieve on your own. Your product is now being sold by reps who have established trusted relationships with customers who believe that the products they are selling are a safe choice.

You also benefit from the large company's indirect sales network of distributors, dealers, resellers, VARs (value-added retailers), and other channel partners. All of these can be leveraged to provide and extend sales reach, installation services, customization capabilities, and customer support.

Leverage an Existing Brand: Along with a large sales force comes brand recognition and reputation. Large companies invest millions of dollars to build and promote their brand. Each year, companies like Apple and Amazon compete for a position in the list of the top ten "world's most valuable" brands, with values worth into the many billions of dollars.

Brand value cannot be underestimated, particularly if you are a small company with limited brand presence. A recognized brand not only delivers name recognition, it also delivers a perception of quality, consistency and trust. It can make the difference between why a customer purchases your product over the competitor's offering.

Understanding the Value You Bring to the Table

A smaller company typically attracts the interest of a large partner by filling a gap in technology. It could be an add-on component that increases functionality, or a complementary product designed to be bundled together as a single solution. Mark Zuckerberg, Facebook's founder, for example, surprised the tech world in 2010 by acquiring the two-year-old startup Instagram for $1 billion. Some suggested he overpaid in order to snap up the popular mobile photo-sharing technology before anyone else could. Whether or not that was the case, Zuckerberg clearly wanted to fill a technology gap and stop a potential competitive threat by buying the innovative photo-sharing app, which has since thrived.

Crystal Decisions faced a similar opportunity. The Crystal report writer was an enhancement to Visual Basic. The combined solution was so successful that within a few years, most developers that purchased Visual Basic were also using Crystal Reports.

Filling a gap doesn't merely apply to software. Examples abound of hardware companies that sell their products containing third-party components. Each provides a complementary benefit and promotes each other's brand.

This was apparent in the early days of desktop computers when there was bundling of "light" software, such as virus and browser applications. Today it's more common for hardware to be sold with a limited use or "freemium" version that can be upgraded (for example, Apple's cloud storage, Dropbox, and Google Drive). This kind of bundling extends beyond tech companies, of course. Cars today are sold with premium brand sound systems and navigation apps, while satellite radios come with a subscription to a satellite communication service, and game systems like PlayStation®4 come bundled with popular games.

Testing the Waters, Knowing When to Pivot

It's not easy to create an airtight business case when considering a strategic partnership, particularly if you are in an industry based on the cutting edge of technology. There are no solid proof points—just a lot of what I like to call "back-of-the-envelope" calculations. The market data you typically require ahead of making a decision may not even exist. With so many unknowns, optimistic assumptions have to be made. These assumptions can often leave those around you with an uneasy feeling unless you can find a way to "test the waters."

Partnering gives both partners an effective way to see if a product might gain traction. So pick one or two value propositions you believe are the winners, then pitch your idea to potential partners (or customers). The larger company may have deeper market insights to offer or, through its distribution channels, can provide a fast feedback loop for new ideas.

Testing may help you settle on a solid value proposition, or at least uncover the best way to pivot the idea into something even more successful.

When working with the technology startup Partnerpedia, our team first approached Cisco with the product we had built for partner portals. Partnerpedia had enjoyed some success with Microsoft and Blackberry, but we believed that adding Cisco to our customer roster would enhance our market credibility. As it turned out, Cisco had no interest in partner portals, but in the course of our meetings with them they suggested they might be interested in an enterprise app store. Partnerpedia launched the cloud-based Enterprise AppZone solution in 2011, then sold it to major customers, including Avaya, VMWare, Cisco, and Coca-Cola.

FINDING WINNERS THOUGH INDUSTRY PIVOTS

There are many examples of "industry pivots," which are typically created when a new technology product has been "tested" by the actual users in the marketplace.

YouTube, for instance, was launched on Valentine's Day 2005 as a video dating site. Almost from the beginning, the founders could see that their original idea was not working as they had envisioned. But when one user used the site to post a funny video ("Me at the Zoo"), they saw how they might "pivot" the idea and focus on simply sharing videos online. Their "pivoted" idea became a runaway success. When YouTube was eventually acquired by Google, the stock value was around $1.65 billion.

Groupon is an example of a good idea that initially was directed at the wrong target market. Founded in 2006, The Point (its original name) was developed as a platform to mobilize groups of people toward action for various social and political causes. The original idea never caught on. Before long, its founder, Andrew Mason, and his investors were headed toward bankruptcy. To save the company, they focused on one aspect of the platform— the coupon/daily deal. Users loved the "pivoted" idea, and the rest is history. Groupon became known as the fastest-growing billion-dollar company in history.[3]

Dancing with Elephants

There's often fear around a boardroom table that the larger company might try to poke its nose inside the tent to figure out your secret sauce and then take your good idea and implement it on its own. This could happen. But an idea on its own, no matter how brilliant, is just an idea. This kind of thinking fails to acknowledge the value in being able to *execute*. It's an aversion to risk that may stand in the way of a successful partnership that can open new doors and deliver strong levels of value and profits.

Similarly, large companies are not necessarily your direct competitors in any way, shape, or form. Typically, they may be slower to market and slower on the innovation curve, compared to smaller companies, since they have other issues to wrestle with. However, they offer brand safety and/or product scalability as a tradeoff.

As the smaller, faster, up-and-coming player, the market expects that you offer more innovative products. It is your responsibility as a smaller company to stay ahead of the curve, move fast, and prove that you can fill what they are missing. But first you have to get noticed.

Think of a large company as an elephant. The company is barely aware you are in the room. There's a great risk that you might get trampled if you *don't* reach out to partner. In short, it's better to know the direction the elephant is going so that you can avoid getting crushed. Focus on the green space of opportunity (where the elephant isn't stepping), which is where you can add customer value.

At Crystal Decisions, for example, we talked about the risk that Microsoft would one day simply copy our report writer idea. But we also joked that it was probably #101 on its list of 100 priorities. We reasoned that as long as we delivered a good-enough product and a good-enough service, swapping out our product with its own would fall below Microsoft's list of priorities to execute.

That's exactly what happened. We did hear that there were initiatives inside Microsoft to build its own report writer. We merely forged ahead. Our goal was to make Microsoft's experience with our company so good that the "elephant" would keep delaying its "switch and replace" decision and continue on with our existing OEM partnership—which in fact it did. Microsoft eventually launched a whole suite of tools like SQL Server Reporting Services (SSRS), but by then, Crystal Decisions had already achieved its goals of market share and brand awareness. In fact, long after Microsoft sold this competing product, the Crystal bundles remained within the Microsoft products. Mission accomplished!

OPENING UP TO GROW A NETWORK

In 2014, Elon Musk surprised everyone by sharing some of Tesla's patents for everyone to use or copy. Musk defended his decision in several ways, noting, first and foremost, that in order for the electric car industry to grow, "the world would all benefit from a common, rapidly evolving technology platform."

Although there is debate over Musk's true motives in giving away the intellectual property in this way, his reasoning is worth noting. He saw Tesla's success as being directly connected to the growth of the electric car industry as a whole, and in order to support both the industry growth and Tesla, there needed to be a powerful "network" effect from outside partners.

"In order for Tesla to succeed," Musk remarked shortly after the initial announcement, "a lot of complementary knowledge and infrastructure needs to be developed. Auto mechanics need to learn how to repair electric vehicles; drivers need to learn to drive and to maintain them; new marketing and distribution channels need to emerge; and the roads need to be populated with charging stations for long distance travelers."[4]

Musk also noted in a YouTube interview, as only he can, that he truly believed it was important to have more electric cars in the world: "If Tesla succeeds and [the] climate is destroyed, it doesn't help Tesla!"

Keeping Eyes Focused on the Big Picture

Partnering is not a short-term game. It may take years to realize the full benefits of a partnership, particularly when the benefits are expected to lead to a significant brand enhancement, a distribution increase, or a possible investment or acquisition. When considering a partnering strategy, stakeholders want to know how normal day-to-day business is going to proceed until the fruits of the strategic partnership are harvested. These questions include both the time and the resources to sustain the company until sales cover the upfront costs, and then how to leverage the initial investment into something that is profitable.

Various remedies can address these concerns. For example, you might include a clause in the partnership contract that covers some of the upfront costs. In the case of Crystal Decisions, company leadership accepted the fact that there were two phases to the business model. Phase one was designed to make it easier for OEM partners to do business with Crystal Decisions. We gave away the original software at a flat rate but without a commission or royalty. We provided tech support for Microsoft's Virtual Basic clients. The strategy was successful in getting Crystal Reports (standard version) bundled with Microsoft Visual Basic, though it meant that Crystal Decisions didn't make any money during this initial phase.

The next phase, however, delivered a return on investment. Part of the deal with Microsoft included the rights to do blind mailings against the Microsoft Visual Basic customer list. Once Crystal Decisions gained the trust of its partners' customers with the initial product, it was able to leverage customer confidence and upsell Crystal Reports Professional. The Pro version included additional features such as accessing and integrating other sources of information beyond the Visual Basic data. This is when Crystal began to make a profit from the product.

Risks of Not Partnering

When Mark Zuckerberg of Facebook was asked about the best advice he'd ever received, he replied, "In a world that's changing so quickly, the biggest risk you can take is not taking any risk."[5]

If you are looking to kick-start higher growth, strategic partnering definitely can be the answer. Are there risks? You bet! But there are also risks in *not* acting. The last and perhaps most important consideration when looking at partnering is the question: "What if we *don't* partner?"

Failure to look for a strategic partner can have an impact on your company beyond immediate sales. Take a look at what competitors might be eyeing. Are they looking at the same opportunity? If you pass on a partnering opportunity, you may discover that your competitor ends up with their software installed on millions of desktops and devices around the world instead of yours. This kind of lost opportunity could be devastating—the difference between winning and losing the market.

Greg Kerfoot, president of Crystal Decisions through the decade when the company grew from $2 million to $250 million in revenues,[6] would often speak of this kind of marketplace competition in terms of "scarcity." His approach instilled in those around him the strong belief that losing a deal means losing it *twice*—once when your company doesn't get the deal and the second time when your competitor scoops the deal.

"There is only going to be one product that wins out there," Kerfoot would tell us, "and if it's not yours, it's going to belong to your competitor. You don't get the deal, and, even worse, they *do* get the deal. Not only are you knocked back, but someone else gets bumped forward. It's not just bad. It's double-bad!"

CHAPTER 2:

CHOOSING YOUR PARTNERS

"If you do not seek out allies and helpers, then you will be isolated and weak."

–Sun Tzu, *The Art of War*

Your entrepreneurial technology company is ready to grow with a product you're certain no one else has developed as well as you have. In fact, you're pretty certain that any large IT company out there would be lucky to have you.

But you are a smaller enterprise, perhaps with fewer than 500 employees,[7] or you're a startup with just a handful of people. Even if you are midsize, the giants out there like Microsoft or SAP most likely don't know who you are. Your sales are modest by large company standards, and you have little or no market presence. Even if you have the next great product ready to go, making even a small dent in the software universe is going to take a lot more than sheer will-power and optimism. All these factors lead to a decision to look for strategic partners. The question is, who?

Begin with a White Board Exercise

As with any good business planning exercise, begin with the goal in mind. Gather together the strategic thinkers in your business. Using the combined market and business intelligence around the table, kick around ideas that would be game-changers for your business. Start listing the big companies you feel could help get you to that next level, or even beyond.

In general, a smaller company should look for large partners. Partnerships with companies of a similar size as yours often do not make a significant enough change in brand awareness or in sales and marketing prospects. There might be exceptions to this, so explore the possibilities. Are there opportunities where you could combine forces on product development? Is there a company in an adjacent market (or a completely different one) where you could leverage each other's technology and assets?

Typical partners for smaller companies might include industry leaders—those "big players" in your space that add significant credibility to the company and the product. Yet partners in complementary or adjacent industries such as hardware manufacturers should also be considered.

For now, don't worry about how difficult or realistic the partnership is. This is the time for big-picture planning and classic "thinking outside the box."

Use a variety of means to search for partnership opportunities: existing contact networks (suppliers, research partners), specialized industry organizations, associations, conference speakers, and trade shows. As you develop a list of potential partners, add individuals' names beside the companies. Those to include might be the CEO, the CTO, Product Managers, VPs of Sales and Marketing, and knowledgeable board members.

Eliminate any companies where there is a specific known reason why partnership at this point in time would not be feasible. For example, if IBM has recently bought a company with a competing product, you might take it off the list. Or if you know for a fact that a certain company—say, Oracle—almost never uses outside partners, remove it from consideration.

WHAT KIND OF PARTNER DO YOU NEED?

For the smaller company:

- Which companies are the leaders in your industry and have the kind of marketing clout to get your product noticed by a much larger market?
- Are there marketing partners that could give you greater geographic and vertical reach?
- Which large company's product would significantly benefit by having your own product's capabilities—for example, fill in their gaps?
- Is there a partner that would make your product a valued vertical solution?
- Are there implementation partners that could extend and accelerate your ability to grow in the market because your own services team isn't yet at capacity?
- Are there service partners who are industry experts that could help you become more valuable to your customers?

For the larger company:

- Which company could help make your product more useful to customers? More complete? More convenient to buy?
- What kind of features or functionality do you want to add into your overall offering that customers might find more valuable? Or, at least, to add in in the short term? This is where you might brainstorm about companies with products that could be bundled with yours to provide a more complete solution.
- Does your competitor have a product or a feature in that product that you'd like to neutralize by adding a partner product to your platform?
- Are there areas of innovation that you could leapfrog or new partners you could attract that would help you beyond your current growth map?

Find Opportunities in the Gaps

Ideally, a strategic partnership happens because there is a two-way need. As we saw in chapter 1, a smaller company is looking to benefit from that company's brand, market awareness, and much larger sales force. The large company is looking for a partner that could augment an existing product or fill a technology gap. For example, they may be seeking an enhancement that would increase product functionality and, in doing so, create enough differentiation to beat its competition.

Identify these kinds of gaps by doing a partial SWOT analysis exercise (Strengths, Weaknesses, Opportunities, Threats), but conduct the analysis from the perspective of a potential partner. Match the gaps you've identified with the value you bring to the table.

Think, in particular, about how you can provide this "next best thing" for a potential partner—the innovation it is looking for to compete or meet a new target market.

FILLING A GAP TO WIN

When it became clear that large companies needed to provide smartphone technology, many looked to outside OEM manufacturers to provide the hardware and to smaller technology partners to help with innovation. This is how the small Taiwanese-based, smartphone manufacturer HTC caught the attention of Google. Google wanted to have access to HTC's 2,000 engineers, known at the time to comprise one of the best smartphone research and development teams in the world.[8] To fill an "R&D" gap in its own enterprise and quickly move ahead in the smartphone space with its Pixel phone lineup, Google acquired the company.

Get Inside of a Partner's Head

Take a moment to get "inside the head" of a large company and consider why strategic partnerships can be so valuable to it. Typically, large companies are busy serving their customers by meeting more traditional needs. They know there are innovations and opportunities worth pursuing, but it is difficult for them to drop what they are doing and make their move. They are committed to legacy systems and requirements, and are bound by process, due diligence, and managing risk. No one is rewarded for sticking their neck out in such companies. In fact, a career-limiting move could be charging down some technology path too soon and skipping all the necessary protocols.

As a result, although large companies talk a lot about innovation, they usually are not the best environment for invention or entrepreneurship.

Innovation is a significant part of the value you bring as an entrepreneurial company. Technology today seems to shift at the speed of light. The ability to create and bring new ideas to fruition is a huge part of why you have appeal as a strategic partner. This applies not just to the product you are pitching today, but also to your value as a partner going forward. Unencumbered by any kind of baggage and history, your product developers can try out different things, see what sticks, learn from mistakes, and take on bigger risks.

Do the Analysis

Use the grid below for your analysis. Rank partnering priorities in each area on a scale of 1 to 10. Add in the value you bring to the table. Then list potential strategic partners and evaluate each relative to those areas. Note the risk points for each side and areas of overlap. In "risk factors," note challenges such as confidentiality and discretion, or any other areas that could bog down discussions and negotiations.

Ultimately, your goal is to come up with a prioritized list of potential strategic partner names to help to focus your efforts. As you narrow down your list, you will also develop a more defined idea as to the kind of partnership you'd prefer: technology, marketing, or sales.

STRATEGIC PARTNERING ANALYSIS

Potential Strategic Partners	Risk Factors	Areas of Overlap	Value You Bring	Score in Terms of Meeting Priorities
e.g., Google	May be developing a competing product	Both are investing in transportation apps	Have a track record and a process for getting ideas implemented quickly	3

WHY DO THE BIG GUYS NEED YOU?

- Your ideas and innovation
- You'll add product functionality they are missing
- Your disruptive technology
- Your ability to be more nimble
- They'll have a way to match or beat their competitors

WHY DO YOU NEED THE BIG GUYS?

- Access to new markets, sales leads, distribution channels, and channel partners
- A larger sales force with geographic and vertical reach
- National/international marketing and brand leverage
- Complementary technology and/or development capabilities

Kinds of Technology Partnerships

Various kinds and levels of technology partnerships exist. Individual companies will have their own specific way of defining and naming tiers of technology partnerships. For example, AWS (Amazon Web Services) refers to levels as Registered, Standard, or Advanced. Depending on the tier, there are expectations to be met on either side. A lower-tier partnership may not seem ideal at first, yet it can be a foot in the door. Once your product is tested, you are in a better position to negotiate a higher level.

"Basic" technology partner is a type of channel partner where a smaller company aligns with a larger manufacturer or producer in order to market and sell its technologies. This is usually done through a co-branding relationship in which the large manufacturer "acknowledges" your product as the preferred one to consider.

"Acknowledged" or **"Authorized" technology partners** of a large IT company, such as Cisco, greatly extend the credibility of your company. When you talk with prospective clients, you can promote your product using the name and brand of the respected large company. Your product is also listed with the large company's products, according to agreed terms.

Certified technology partners are a form of higher-tiered technology partnership typically recognized by a logo or certificate you can use on all your marketing materials (e.g., "Intel Inside"). Certification provides an added level of trust in functionality for potential clients. When you are a certified partner, customers can be assured that your product and software integration claims are sound. Certification by SAP, for example, tells an SAP customer that you are a safe choice.

Each of these technology partnerships usually has a time and money requirement associated with the level. Certification for products requires engineering resources and often mandates a lab test to verify functionality. Certification for service providers requires specific training and often an exam at the end. There may be various levels, depending on the requirements (for example, premier, silver, and gold).

Beyond certification, there still is no guarantee that a larger company is actually going to help a smaller partner sell more of the product. However, the IT industry is famous for being a certification-centric industry. Getting the "seal of approval" from Amazon, Microsoft, Cisco, and others no doubt provides valuable product differentiation as well as a marketing advantage.

Marketing partnerships are alliances that ideally benefit both partners. A large company such as Salesforce agrees to go to market with your company and promote your product because it is a way of expanding its solution and making its company more competitive than, say, Oracle. Marketing partnerships can produce game-changing results for both companies. The smaller company achieves much wider marketing awareness and branding than it could ever achieve on its own. And the large company increases its sales exponentially. (See example below, about Unidesk and Dell.)

With a marketing partnership in place, the two marketing departments ostensibly work together. In reality, it is the large company's department that typically provides most, if not all, of the direction.

Sales partnerships are often viewed as the ultimate partnership. In a sales partnership, your product appears on the large company's price list, which means customers can purchase it directly from the larger company and/or its distribution channels. This is a clear indication that the large company wants your product as part of a total solution. Sales partnership can take the form of lead referral, cooperation on sales deals, or ultimately listing of your product on its price list.

Consider, for example, a salesperson in the field trying to close a multi-million-dollar deal with Proctor & Gamble. Say that P&G requires a particular add-on, which it doesn't have, and as it happens your company's product is listed in its book as an outside vendor solution. In this instance, the salesperson is fully confident in recommending the product. Once recommended, the client doesn't even question whether or not to purchase your product; they see it as part of their "total solution."

MOVING UP PARTNERSHIP "TIERS"

The story of Unidesk reads as a real strategic partnership dream. Launched in 2008, the small Massachusetts-based startup is the inventor of the groundbreaking Windows application packaging and management technology known as "layering."

In 2012, the IT giant Dell was looking to fill a gap in its offering. It added Unidesk's Desktop Virtualization Solutions to its product lineup by agreeing to a lower-level technology partnership with Unidesk. At the time Unidesk had about 215 clients.

After two years, Unidesk proved itself to be a worthy partner. It "moved up" to be one of Dell's first four "Tier 1" partners. Both sides gained substantially as a result of their combined go-to-market strategy. Unidesk experienced huge growth, while Dell sold significantly more product. In fact, for every dollar in revenue Unidesk earned on a sale, Dell earned $10. As a result, Dell began to send referrals to Unidesk, one in three of which typically turned into customers for Unidesk.

In 2017, Citrix acquired Unidesk for an undisclosed sum in order to stay ahead in an extremely competitive "virtual" market.

Move the Mountain

Large companies usually don't come to you. Alas, you are just a small fish in a big pond. Your product could be the best in the world, but sometimes you have to move the mountain yourself. This is perhaps the toughest message for a company with a great product to appreciate.

First, you have to find ways to let the big guys in the industry know you exist, and then keep pushing forward. Once a large company knows who you are and what you offer, they will be watching you and looking for ways to gain from the value you bring. Ideally, this may be a strategic partnership; however, at some point they may want more. They may, for instance, view the product you are offering in a strategic partnership as competition to a similar product in its own business. That is perfectly okay. The rewards of the larger company's wanting to take over your idea completely can be substantial if you negotiate the right deal. If it's the right partner, the benefit to your business should greatly outweigh the threat of competition.

Second, moving the mountain is really hard to do. It takes time and money, with no immediate guarantee of success. Once you've got at least a partial list, you need to start meeting potential partners, asking questions, continually gaining market intelligence, and uncovering the gaps. Remember: Don't stop just because you've had a couple of successes. Follow all leads. When you come across a block or a "gatekeeper," make them your friend. Consider all information as good information. Accept the fact that it will take countless emails, conversations, and meetings before something sticks.

Getting traction on your initial inquiries, setting up the first meetings, and moving along negotiations are all exciting parts of putting together a strategic partnership. But only time will tell which partnerships will yield the best results or will lead to great opportunities.

ZERO TO 10,000 CLIENTS IN TWO YEARS, STEP-BY-STEP

TrialPay is a prime example of a company that shot from zero to 10,000 clients in two years through a relentless process that started with a list and a system for prioritizing its choices.[9]

Led by CEO Alex Rampell, TrialPay built an ecommerce payment system that gave consumers the option to try out other products or services for free when they were buying something else.

As Rampell launched his company in 2006, he created a potential list with contacts his team knew, including family and friends as well as known business targets. A few small partners in the software vertical market were added, including WinZip, because that company was owned by an acquaintance of Rampell's. The team then set out to clarify the type of partners they needed to be working with outside their industry in order to reach their ideal customers and brands. TrialPay's business development team asked, "Who are the partners that can deliver us the hottest new leads?"

The research produced a list of web merchants and companies that they work with. Then TrialPay prioritized the names by doing an analysis using a basic matrix, with feasibility on the x-axis and possible benefit on the y-axis. A company called Download.com was identified as a perfect fit: a trusted, safe site for software, mobile, and game applications. By signing Download.com, TrialPay gained access to some

60,000 merchants it could never have reached on its own. Yet Rampell didn't stop there.

"Our business development team went to every other download site on the planet, including many that you've probably never heard of," Rampell said in an interview. "And it was even easier to get to them because we could say, 'Download.com is one of our biggest channel partners. Do you want the same deal? We can pay you a lot.' "

TrialPay continued to push forward. The company cinched partnership deals with almost every major consumer software company. In doing so, the e-commerce upstart totally shut out its competition, and in 2015 Visa acquired it for an undisclosed amount.

CHAPTER 3:

LET'S MAKE A DEAL

"Negotiating is a basic means of getting what you want from others. It is back-and-forth communication designed to reach an agreement when some interests are shared and others are opposed.

Communicate loudly and convincingly things you are willing to say that the other side would like to hear; this can give them real incentive to reach agreement on other issues."

–Roger Fisher and William Ury, *Getting to Yes*

In an interview, Dropbox cofounder Drew Houston talks about what it was like in 2009 when he and his partner were "summoned" to Apple headquarters in Silicon Valley. Houston was 27 at the time and looking for the right partnership opportunity. After being "kicked up the food chain" they finally landed a meeting with Steve Jobs. "So we went into the boardroom," says Houston, "and you're looking around the walls, and it's just this pantheon of all the Mac products or all the Apple products over the years, you know, from the original Mac onward, maybe even before. And so everybody sits down, and he [Jobs] leans back in his chair and he's like, 'Where to begin?'"[10]

Although Houston ended up famously turning Job's offer down (Jobs wanted to make Dropbox part of Apple), his experience tells something about what can happen when a smaller player makes the right connection with the right people, and in doing so, catches the attention of a big player—the actual elephant in the room.

Up until now, you've likely only imagined what it would be like to land a meeting with a company like Apple or Amazon. But now you are ready to make it happen. Like others who've negotiated strategic partnerships, you don't know at this point where the discussions might lead. What you *do* know is that you need to get in front of a senior executive or product manager in order to make your case.

So, in Steve Jobs' words, "Where to begin?"

Mine Your Networks

The search for a strategic partner typically begins by looking up the websites of companies you've identified in chapter 2, then identifying management team members and understanding the organizational structure of the company. Prepare a spreadsheet with job titles, contact information, and additional notes you've researched about each specific company. You'll also want a column to record your progress once you start. The more prepared you are ahead of time and the more information about contacts you can amass, the better your chances of success.

Other tips for identifying potential contacts include:

- Set up Google alerts for companies so you can keep tabs on them, their recent developments, and their news announcements.

- LinkedIn groups, potential partners' user forums, and blogs are other ways to determine what's happening with their partner community and the challenges or pain points they may be facing.

- Scour your various networks, such as LinkedIn, to see if anyone at the target company has a common connection with you so that you can ask for an introduction.

- Conferences can be great places to find leaders in specific product areas. After attending a session, march right up and introduce yourself, then follow up to schedule a meeting.

Understand Your Target Audience

You'll want to start with product managers or whoever owns the product management function. By job definition, product managers own the responsibility of the "whole product"—that is, the feature set, the go-to-market strategy, and the profit/loss potential. By nature, these managers are also highly analytical, with a good understanding of both business and technical issues. This unique combination of technical plus business and marketing savvy positions them as the proper point persons for all interests: technical, engineering, support, sales, and marketing.

In large companies, however, there could be hundreds of people with product management responsibility, and within each product management group even layers of hierarchy: for example, VPs of product management, product directors, and senior product managers who oversee a specific product or part of a product. Many product managers may already have identified areas where partnerships would be welcomed, to accelerate sales and marketing competitiveness.

Other department heads are also worth considering:

- A vice president of sales is often painfully aware of where he or she is losing deals, and therefore may need your help with product features or technology enhancements.

- A vice president of engineering is also keenly aware of product areas that are missing features. Take note, however, that those in the engineering group may be less willing to partner. You could experience push-back because the VP prefers to hire more engineers instead of bringing in a partner, which could lead to losing control of the development process, thereby creating dependencies.

Making the Pitch

The end goal is to open up a meeting with the right person—ideally, the CEO or a strategic product manager. The "ask" is an introductory phone call or a meeting to explore mutual value.

Prepare an email that catches the reader's attention. The message should be no more than a brief paragraph that outlines who you are, why you are interested in them as a partner, and how you can add value.

A little research goes a long way in helping a large company believe that you are worth the time and risk. Identify "hot" areas of interest based on feedback from analysts and market reports. Dangle any nuggets of worth, such as specific industry insight that increases your value as an innovative, plugged-in company in the eyes of the other party. Ideally, you have uncovered through research and conversations that the larger company is facing a major threat from a competitor. Point out how partnering might be exactly what it would take to help topple their competition. The partnership could take the form of a joint alliance where the smaller company gains much-needed marketing support in exchange for a technology add-on—a product that would give them first-entrant advantage.

POP UP ABOVE THE NOISE

Send a 150- to 200-word email written to attract attention, detailing:

- Who you are
- What company you represent
- What your company does (brief and to the point)
- What your "secret sauce" is (no more than three points)
- What strategic value your product would bring to their company
- A call to action: "Can we meet next Tuesday at 10:30 a.m.?"

Push, Prod, and Persevere

At this point, the process might feel like you are throwing spaghetti at the wall to see what sticks. Keep at it because eventually you'll start getting some traction. You are trying to connect with some of the busiest people in huge, perhaps global companies, dealing with multiple incoming requests and ideas. Consider these suggestions:

- Don't limit yourself to one person or those in very senior positions. As an outsider, it is difficult for you or your colleagues to figure out what's going on inside a company in areas such as current product development, where the buck stops, who and what is driving initiatives and priorities, and so forth.

- Send two or three messages to different contacts at the company to increase your odds of getting a successful reply.

- Sometimes the timing is wrong. Perhaps the product manager is just a week away from a product launch. Look at the company's tradeshow schedule or find someone who can give you information on how you can take advantage of the planning cycle next time, when the next big launch events take place, and even who sets the schedule.

- You may need to push for a clear answer so that you know you are not wasting someone's time (or if they are wasting *yours*). Know when to clearly state, "if you are not interested at all, let me know and I'll go away." This can force a decision. Similarly, you can always ask if there is someone else you should be talking to, to get a different lead. Being bounced around can often lead to new areas of interest.

Don't Stop at One

Even when you get a positive response from one company, you still want to be pitching to others. You don't know which companies are going to be successful and which products will be winners in the long term.

Talk with everyone who fits your priorities as a strong lead, and dig out as much information as you can. If you can get more than one meeting booked with your chosen contact, you will be better informed going into a negotiation, and therefore more valuable as a contact.

Move each inquiry along, keeping an eye on your priorities as well as where you are getting the strongest interest. Look at the big players but don't ignore the midsize ones. As your knowledge and network expands, you can be more strategic in your negotiations. Landing a partnership deal with a vendor that's considered "number one" in the market should become a priority. This gives you terrific leverage, because it encourages competing vendors to want your product in order to neutralize any major competitors.

Your goal is to sign up as many partnership deals as possible. You may have to set some priorities, but as long as you stay on top of what's going on, juggling multiple projects is always going to be a good problem to have.

That "Magic" Moment

Okay, so you've booked your first meeting. This is a good first step, but it's only when you've booked a *second* meeting that you've passed the sniff test. This is the moment in every sales cycle when suddenly you are moving from lead generation to realistic prospects.

Another telltale sign can be who's now in the room. When you arrive for that second or third meeting, the boss's boss may be there, or a larger group of senior people ready to check you out. Now you *really* know they are paying attention. The large company is taking a deeper dive and figures it's time to take a more nitty-gritty look at what could be done.

You may find that one or more of these internal contacts will start to champion you. This is another very positive sign. They may share information to help you be successful when you meet others on the team; they may offer advice on how to navigate within the company; they may let you in on internal politics or hint at how you can align with their internal product planning cycles and priorities.

You also may be asked during these early discussions if you are speaking to other companies. Be upfront about your goals. There is no harm in letting potential partners know at this stage that you are not solely focused on them. In fact, it creates a sense of urgency because of the scarcity effect.

NON-DISCLOSURE AGREEMENTS (NDA)

At any point during these early meetings you may be asked to sign an NDA. This is a common business practice. By signing an NDA, participants promise to not divulge or release information shared with them by the other people involved. You should carefully read what you sign and make sure that the NDA is mutual—that is, that both parties are making disclosures and are bound to keep each other's disclosures secret, unless given permission to do otherwise. Examine the terms carefully, as NDAs can differ. If you can afford it, have legal counsel review the terms, such as when the agreement expires, and whether confidential matters are required to be expressed in writing after a meeting for them to be deemed as such.

The Art of Negotiation

In business terms, negotiations have now started. True, you are still dancing (cautiously) with a ten-thousand-pound elephant, but it is becoming clear that you have something to offer. You job is to make this potential partner see that value and keep talking with you.

Negotiation is a matter of style. It can vary in terms of what makes sense in each particular case. Those leading the negotiation may choose to focus more on the value at stake, as in: *Here's how our product can make more profits for your customers.* Others focus more on fear: *If you miss this opportunity, we'll partner with your competitor and you'll be left behind in their dust.* In general, fear is a bigger motivator than greed.

"Sign this non-disclosure agreement
— I'm going to use a secret recipe."

Keep in mind that for the large company, this is probably just one deal among many; for your company, though, it could be the deal that makes or breaks your future. You don't want to be openly threatening but you *do* want to show that you are savvy. You are not just selling your product, you are selling your company: You have a strong management team, a clear vision, and an aptitude for innovation with a strong development team. You're not going to stand around and wait for things to happen. If your target company doesn't take you up on the partnership, you are going to push forward with someone else and make waves in the market.

This is all part of why you are an attractive partner for them. In short, you may be smaller than they are, but they sense you are determined to be a winner in the market—a force to be reckoned with.

FROM HUMBLE BEGINNINGS TO GLOBAL TRANSPORTATION LEADER

UberCab started with Travis Kalanick's idea for hailing a car by using a smartphone. When Uber was still a small upstart, Kalanick's belief in strategic partnering led him to consider contacting Google to pursue a strategic partnership around its maps, GPS, and other resources.

The resulting partnership gave Uber much more. In 2013, Google invested $258 million in the company. This fuelled the company's rapid expansion. But the deal was beneficial to both the small startup and the giant Google.

Because of the partnership, Uber became the only ride-sharing company listed by Google as an option. This gave Uber access to more customers than it ever could have reached otherwise. It also gave the company the ability to win more market share. In return, Uber continued to rely heavily on Google technology, and allowed Google Maps to enhance the utility of its features for the users. For the time being, at least, this helped Google stay ahead of competitors by being aligned with the global leader in the transportation industry.

Uber continued building partnerships that included Internet companies in China, auto manufacturers, grocery giants, and even entertainment platforms like Spotify and NBC Sports, to mention only a few. Through such partnerships, it has since spread around the globe, with operations in approximately 60 countries and a value of over $60 billion.

A Deal Starts to Take Shape

Initially, you would work out an outline in business terms. This could be a verbal agreement, or a one-page written document that describes the nature of the deal at a high level: which product(s), the plans for distribution, and some idea as to compensation. At this stage, the large company may ask for a proposal, or may put a draft agreement into its standard template.

It's better at this stage to focus on where the value lies instead of getting bogged down by price specifics. However, it *is* wise to have a general discussion about compensation. Try to avoid big surprises later on. Talk about similar deals you've put together, and feel out what the large company may be thinking of in terms of price and economic terms.

Setting Realistic Expectations

As these business discussions progress, it is essential to talk up front about what success might look like once you've got the partnership up and running. This calls for realistic analysis, not just blue-sky visioning. Measuring results can be difficult when there have been overly high expectations as to what the partnership might achieve or, in many instances, how quickly those positive results materialize.

This is particularly the case for sales projections. It is very common to see overly optimistic numbers in the early stages of a business negotiation. After all, it's likely one of the main reasons that the partnership idea attracted excitement in the first place. But, in the months to come, unrealistic sales goals can pose a real problem for both sides. The smaller company most likely banked on how much revenue would be generated. The larger company might have convinced other senior executives in the enterprise to support the deal, based on a much larger number of additional units predicted to sell. It's no wonder that sales goals are at the top of the list in terms of misaligned expectations.

A smart way to avoid this scenario is to have a frank discussion about minimum and maximum projections. Although the conversation may start at a high level, insist on granular detail to nail down exactly what is being recommended. It's hard enough within a company's own financial unit to get a good discussion around budgets. When you're sorting it out with another company, such discussions can be difficult and can often be considered to contain proprietary and confidential information.

Take time to pull out the information. There may be pride involved, or partners who may not want to be totally transparent about their total financials, but getting all the information is worthwhile in the end. These kinds of questions (and answers) give both sides more confidence in the validity of the numbers: How many phone calls are going to be coming into the tech support lines, based on the units projected to be sold? Is this plausible, based on the orders you have projected, and do the expenses cover the costs? What do the sales projections look like? What does big sales success look like? What are the minimum numbers expected? What is the midpoint?

Resource allocation is another area that requires a realistic analysis: Who's going to be doing the integration and development, who's doing the training, who's providing the tech support, who's doing the marketing, and who's going to do the selling?

Doing this kind of pre-work also brings up some hard rubber-meets-the-road discussions, such as commitments to vendors. Set realistic expectations for more than one scenario. For example, if you believe you'll ship a million units, you'll have to scale up distribution costs; but what if you only ship half of that? High sales projections for a technology product mean a demand for more resources for customer support and customer service training. What if you gear up with a large customer support team and the sales aren't as good as expected?

Reaching a Business Deal

Once you've had multiple meetings and interacted with various levels of management, a deal starts to take shape. These kinds of business discussions lead both parties toward an actual contract, but you should keep the conversation at a high enough level that both sides can talk frankly without lawyers in the room. This helps the parties keep focused on the mutual value proposition and, ideally, be more creative in envisioning how they see the partnership working successfully. Now is the ideal time to try getting inside the other side's head to anticipate any difficulties in the partnership structure that might interfere with success, and then to frankly name them. Agree ahead of time on what is defined as "success" and how to measure it. Raise all kinds of questions. Be entirely open to listening to what each side needs or the risks they believe they might be facing. Negotiate aggressively and continue to communicate—and agree on—the benefits along the way.

CHAPTER 4:

SIGNING THE CONTRACT

"It is easier to get into trouble than to get out of it."

–Curtis E. Sahakian, Managing Director,
Corporate Partnering Institute

Eventually the dance ends. The business terms of the negotiation agreement begin to include legal terms. This takes you to a more formal phase, leading up to the point when both sides sign a legally binding contract that outlines their responsibilities and financial stake in the partnership.

Now the intricacies can become quite complex. Both sides will have lawyers present: the large company, a team of lawyers; and your smaller company, perhaps in-house counsel or often a lawyer who is part of an extended professional services team.

Be warned: When the lawyers become involved, things can get sticky (and expensive!).

There are multiple structures of strategic partnerships, ranging from non-equity alliances to equity-based partnerships, equity investments, and complex joint ventures. Larger companies will have their own boilerplate versions for each. Going into contract negotiations across the table of a giant company, it is helpful to know some of the "hot spots" you will likely face as the smaller, less powerful partner. *The following is not intended to replace the advice of your own legal team or lawyers.*

Intellectual Property (IP)

Conflict over intellectual property sharing is considered one of the top three reasons why strategic partnerships fail.[11] IP certainly can become one of the trickiest parts of the negotiation.

Each side brings its own fears. Large companies are concerned about IP because they know that by partnering they are giving away ideas that might end up in the hands of a potential competitor. Smaller companies are concerned about their own IP because they are often convinced that it's only a matter of time before a large company tries to steal or copy it.

The best approach is to come to a clear, written understanding that each side owns its own IP, and define a clear API interface to separate each party's code.

If the large partner pushes back, this is a good time to remind those around the negotiating table that it is in *everyone's* best interest that the smaller company remain a healthy, innovative, and independent business. Ownership of your own IP, spelled out in clear terms with defined boundaries, is the reason you'll remain this way. Your IP is also your most valuable asset. If (or when) you exit your business via an acquisition or merger, the buyer will insist on knowing that it is getting your IP free and clear.

Exclusivity

Often the bigger company tries to tie a smaller partner down with an exclusivity agreement. This request is cringe-worthy. The goal of your business is to grow! Locking you into an exclusivity agreement works against your best interest by restraining you from finding more opportunities in the market. It also places the smaller partner at great risk if the partnership deal doesn't work out as planned.

Similar to negotiations around IP, you can counter the request by explaining that it is to everyone's advantage to deal with a viable, growing vendor, not one tied into a risky, single partnership arrangement.

Our first Strategic OEM Partner for Crystal Reports was the huge database company Borland with its flagship product, dBase. Borland seemed like an ideal partner for us at the time. But as it turned out, the Visual Basic deal we made with Microsoft was much better for us. If we'd agreed to an exclusive with Borland, we would have failed as a company. We also didn't stop at Microsoft. We built a massive channel of over 150 strategic OEM partnerships that included the "who's who" of the software world. In the end, our product became an industry standard for report writers.

Time-Delay Exclusive

A variation on the above asks for a time delay before you can sell to other vendors. This comes from a fear that somehow the large company might lose a portion of the market to competitors.

As stated above, remind the large company that it is critical that you remain a strong, sustainable business. With its massive distribution channels, it has sales execution capability on its side. It is not likely that you could beat it to market.

In addition, be honest about your intentions. Either confirm with the large company that you are not talking with anyone else, or be clear about whom you are talking to so they are not blindsided.

If you can't eliminate some kind of exclusivity, try for as short a term as possible—perhaps six months or less before the exclusivity clause ends. Another compromise could be an agreement to list just a few vendors that are out of bounds to you, with a time limit.

Up-Front Payments

Make sure you include an up-front payment to cover expenses and lost revenue incurred over the period leading up to the launch and until the time when sales begin to occur.

Smaller enterprises, which are used to working nimbly and efficiently, can be surprised at the amount of additional time involved when working with the larger company once a project begins. There are going to be a lot of distractions as both sides are learning how to work together. You have to account for numerous meetings and the general back-and-forth that takes place to cover what's relevant for each party. Activities that you assume might take two days of development effort could now take a couple of weeks. In addition, there are lost-opportunity costs. While you are consumed with this one project, it may even be difficult to carry on business as usual.

Royalties and Commissions

It might be made clear from the beginning that the larger company does not pay on a per-unit royalty basis and is looking instead for unlimited licensing. This is a good opener for a discussion about how that can protect what is important to the company, while still making the deal attractive to you. For example, you may want to put a mechanism in place to upsell a premium version.

Similar to the Crystal Decisions deal discussed in chapter 1, instead of demanding per-unit royalties, the larger company might provide a blind mailing list of its customers. This strategy could incent the larger company to take a chance on the partnership. The larger company takes the risk that initial sales are not so good as expected; the smaller partner takes the risk upfront that sales will come along down the road through premium upgrade sales.

Source Code

A large company may ask for source code in a contract. It probably was informed that having access to such source code is needed for business continuity. Just tell the lawyers involved that your source code will be of little use to them without the knowledge of the developers who wrote the code. Instead, you can offer it in escrow, with clear terms and conditions as to when the code could be released. This will satisfy the large company's concern that it will be able to continue to support its customers in the event that you go out of business.

Launch and Event Dates

Typically, various trade shows or industry events will take place over the next year where someone senior in the large company—a VP or the CEO—wants to make a major announcement. Additional pressure likely comes from its marketing and public relations departments that need to complete key messaging at least three to four weeks in advance of such events. The looming deadlines usually give your smaller company a huge piece of leverage. Being able to negotiate around key dates can be a major driver for getting a deal done, *and* with terms favorable to your side.

Marketing Communication

Corporate marketing departments at large vendors are extremely strict in terms of controlling their brand. Brand guidelines, for example, put strong restrictions on the sharing of any kind of brand identity. Corporate marketing departments also do very little to assist smaller partners regarding key marketing events and priorities, such as a launch press release or trade show booths. They may even refuse to list partnership names and/or logos on their website and in social media.

Such realities can make it very tough for a smaller partner that expects to benefit from brand exposure. So, as much as possible, negotiate specific terms and marketing asks. Make sure the specifics are written into the contract. Some marketing deliverables could be the following:

- "Large Company A will issue a joint press release announcing the partnership, including the name of the partner."

- "Large Company A will provide trade show booth space at no charge to the partner."

- "Company B can use Large Company A's logo on its website and in promotional materials as long as it follows the style guide as provided by Company A."

Indemnification and Liability

Indemnification is the part of an agreement that provides for one party to bear the monetary costs, either directly or by reimbursement, for losses incurred by a second party. Possibly the most awkward moments in a deal come when lawyers for the large company ask for draconian indemnification terms. When stated in a partnership agreement, it means that the larger company bears no responsibility for anything that goes wrong, and the smaller company takes on all the liability. This is typically stated as unlimited or in the tens of millions of dollars.

When you look at the money at stake in the deal, an indemnification request in millions of dollars is totally out of proportion with the value of the deal. However, indemnification and liability terms can be deal-breakers because of the true mismatch of the powers involved. For the large company, the partnership represents a single transaction, but for the smaller company it is a game-changer.

Having a good lawyer on your side is key because you should *not* agree to these kinds of terms. At this point, something has to give—hopefully, from the senior management's point of view on the other side. With the deal at stake, he or she needs to lower the level of risk for you either by revising the terms or by reducing the liability amount.

Point Persons and Conflict Resolution

Designated point persons need to be named to provide coordination, direction, and authority in technical, development, and business areas. The same people (or others as named) should be assigned to revisit the contract when conflicts arise. Questions to answer include: When is an issue considered "escalated"? to whom? and at what level?

Contract Provisions and Recommendations

The provisions discussed above, as well as the standard provisions you find in a typical partnership agreement, are listed below. Beside each are recommendations on how to negotiate each provision.

PROVISION	RECOMMENDATION
Duration What should the term of the contract be: 1 year; 3–5 years; or longer?	3–5 years is best. If they want a longer term, ask for 3 years with an annual auto-renewal plus a notification time required to end the contract for either side. One year is too short to get anything accomplished.
Product development deadlines and milestones	Set deadlines and expect these will be taken seriously. Specified dates are difficult to adjust once development begins, particularly when tied to a launch event. If possible, however, build in some contingency buffers in case of extreme circumstances that could cause a delay on either side.

PROVISION	RECOMMENDATION
Compensation: price, commissions, and fees Large company makes it clear it does not offer a commission or royalty	If the large company will not pay a commission or royalty fee, state the mechanism by which you intend to secure profits and what you'll need from it to support this strategy (for example, access to customers, "blind" mailing lists, additional access to sales channels, etc.)
Tiered discounts	The contract may specify tiered discounts based on sales volumes. These discounts are influenced by the sales projections that were discussed during the negotiations so ask your team if they seem reasonable.
Upfront payment	Development costs take resources away from your key product initiatives and road map. Make sure you cover upfront costs; e.g., you might ask for $100k, $500k, or $1million up-front fees upon signing.
Point persons and conflict resolution	Name point persons on both sides who will take on responsibility for key areas such as business issues, relationship management, pricing, and technical/development. Specify who has responsibility for conflict resolution, such as how an issue is dealt with and when it's escalated to another level.

PROVISION	RECOMMENDATION
Exclusivity Large company requests that it is your only partner vendor	Do not agree to this. If you cannot get agreement, negotiate a time-limited exclusivity of 6 months or less. A better solution is a time window during which exclusivity only applies to a small set of defined vendors.
Intellectual property Large company requests your IP and APIs	Do not agree to this. Your IP and APIs lie at the core of your company value. Set out agreements as to who owns what, with clear terms and definitions. Each partner should own its own IP separately; if a product is created together, create an interface of APIs and keep each party's code and IP separate.
Source code Large company asks for source code	Do not agree to this. Agree instead to provide the source code in escrow so that the large company is protected in the event you go out of business or cannot fulfill your contract obligations.
Support Large company asks that you provide Tier 1 support	Avoid if you can. You could get swamped with calls because of the mismatch in company size. Instead, offer second- or third-level developer support. Support volumes and liabilities are also affected by sales projections. Make sure your interests are covered, with support obligations set according to the volume of actual sales.

PROVISION	RECOMMENDATION
Marketing Marketing is particularly important for the smaller company; specific requests should be named	Typical "asks" should include: • Joint press release announcing the partnership • Promotion of the partnership at trade shows and events • Inclusion of the company product name with the partner's product, e.g. Crystal Reports for Microsoft Visual Basic (This is a much tougher negotiation compared to completing a white label agreement in which there is no mention of the OEM product.) • Access to customer lists (e.g., blind mailings) • Inclusion of partner name on a website, trade show booth, and other key marketing communication pieces
Training Large company requests extensive training for a very large group of employees in various training channels	Although it is tactical, training can be an important enabler of the partnership. Training falls into two categories: sales and tech support; both can be very costly and resource-intensive for the smaller partner. It is best to negotiate for responsibility to provide train-the-trainer programs and materials where you can leverage the larger company training channels and resources.

PROVISION	RECOMMENDATION
Indemnification and liability Large company requests unreasonable terms	As the partner in the weaker negotiating position, don't get pushed into an unreasonable indemnification agreement. Protect your company from risks by negotiating limits on your liability in terms of what it covers, and the amount.
Exit plan	Circumstances may arise, such as an acquisition or merger, that could put the relationship at risk. You want to be clear in the contract that if this is ever the case, consent to new ownership will not be unreasonably refused. Outline exit plans in advance. Upon acquisition, agree to give the partnering company adequate notice, e.g., 90 days. Specify measures intended to keep the relationship in place if it is to the benefit of both parties.

Contracts Are Only the Beginning

The contract stage can get derailed if those doing the negotiating start prioritizing goals according to their own self-interests rather than those of the partnership. Far too quickly, participants can lose sight of the overall value proposition.

McKinsey supports such findings through research that shows how many ventures fail because they spend more time on steps where less value is at risk and less time on steps that have more value at risk (50 percent of time spent on negotiating deal terms, which constitute only 10 percent of value at risk, and only 20 percent of time spent on business model and structure, which represents around 40 percent of total value at risk).[12]

It is also good to remember at the contract stage that although third-party professionals—for example, lawyers and their staff—play important roles, they are not the ones who have to live with the final results. It is too easy for them to lose a CEO's vision and dominate the process in order to reach their best result of billable hours or an effort to try to mitigate all risks. Keep in mind that these are *their* interests, not necessarily yours. There will be risks in any partnership. The key is to make a business evaluation of those risks.

Success stories abound to remind you that despite the challenges of a negotiation and signing a deal, the end result can be extremely beneficial in the long term.

PARTNERING SUCCESS ONE DEAL AT A TIME

In 2017, David Chait was named "Entrepreneur of the Year" at the ASTA Global Convention in San Diego. This first-time entrepreneur had spent long hours trying to sign a partnership deal with Travefy, the software company he founded that builds itinerary management and client collaboration software for travel professionals and companies.

"Although it was extremely challenging to pin down our first partner," said Chait, referencing the countless meetings and iterations, "once we did so, each subsequent partner was easier and quicker [to acquire]. Now, a little more than a year later, we have partnerships with multiple online travel agents and serve hotel results from hundreds of travel sites to our users."[13]

CHAPTER 5:

LEADING TO THE LAUNCH

"We've had three big ideas at Amazon that we've stuck with for 18 years, and they're the reason we're success-ful: Put the customer first. Invent. And be patient."

–Jeff Bezos, CEO, Amazon

You've done it! The partnership deal has been signed and it's time to celebrate. There's champagne popping, high fives, and back-slapping all around. An announcement is made with much fanfare. Optimism abounds as to what this means for the company. Buzz-words like "game-changer" and "sea change" are tossed about while everyone imagines how great it's going to be now that they're aligned with a large, prestigious partner.

But first, exhaustion sets in. For months you have marshaled all your company's resources to get the task done; you've negoti-ated to the line, even survived the moment when the other side took the proverbial walk to the door. Next, however, there's immedi-ate work to be done. Now that the deal has finally come together, you have to navigate what is clearly going to disrupt business as normal at your company.

The signing of a partnership deal is a major change in direction for a smaller company. The product needs to be launched within a contracted deadline, usually within a year. Enormous pressures are put on the smaller company, and the impact ripples throughout its ranks. Up until now, those working on the deal—typically, the CEO, the product manager, some key engineers, and a few sales and marketing people—knew firsthand what has been going on. But for the rest of the company, it's probably the first time the news is confirmed. Employees at other levels in your organization may be less visionary than top managers and less experienced in working with different bureaucracies and cultures. Those in operations may lack knowledge of the strategic context. The time and resources now being directed at supporting the partnership deal may not seem to make sense to them, in terms of the effort and aggravation.

This chapter deals with what happens leading up to the first product launch, and details the challenges faced inside the company during the first few months of a strategic partnership.

Move from "The Deal" to Actually Working Together

Once both sides start working toward a product launch, reality sets in. Those in senior roles in development, business, sales, and marketing have been intimately involved throughout the process, advising on high-level strategies, goals, and priorities. But now the technical and operational people also must step out of the trenches and work out the granular details related to technical integration, support, and sales and marketing activities. There will be major changes to the product development road map, new processes for sales and marketing, and new systems and tools for training and technical support.

Employees on both sides must sit down with their counterparts and figure out actual work plans, most likely in the face of impossibly tight deadlines. Tasks and projects include looking at systems, security, and processes already in place, deciding what can be used and what needs to be revised or created, and then setting expectations and clear handover points.

Technical people need to meet with their counterparts on the other side and agree on the interfaces, drill down on the features and functionalities, and set milestones. Similarly, those in marketing, sales, and support at the smaller company need to immediately familiarize themselves with how terms negotiated in the contract relate to marketing, sales, and support functions within their areas of responsibility, and determine what action steps need to be taken next to execute on the agreement. On the marketing front, there may be immediate marketing opportunities to plan—typically, the participation at upcoming trade shows, as well as other marketing events in the coming months.

Financial projections have been made in anticipation of a deal, but those in financial roles may now have new details and actuals to review in regard to revenue and expense planning. No doubt there will be requests for added expenses, perhaps to send staff to trade shows or to take advantage of new educational and training opportunities available through the large company. Expenses for everything (from additional staff to a new trade show booth) need to be weighed and prioritized in order to reap the best benefits from the new partnership opportunity.

Typically, there's a "partner community" or a "developer network" in place at the large company where resources, information, and tools are made available to partners. But even using that takes time. One company, for example, signed a partnership deal as an independent software vendor for Salesforce. Its excitement soon diminished when it couldn't connect into the partner community. Between the time when the contract was finalized and getting signed up, the login password it had been provided had expired. At a time when everyone was scrambling to get things done, it took three weeks to get technical and operations staff at the smaller company into the system![14]

Figuring Out Who, What, and When

Those named as point persons in the contract take the lead—typically, these will be separate people for technical project management, customer support, and business and contract issues. Specific staff is assigned to each project area. A development team is assembled solely for technical integration. A marketing coordinator is put in place on the sales and marketing side to leverage the marketing power at the larger company. Internally, its first order of business is to make an internal announcement to its employees. Business development continues to monitor and build the partner relationship.

The general timeline and milestones for the coming year look something like this:

Marketing event: The large company announces the news of the partnership through a press release in order to create buzz in the industry and get press. Unless the format and content of the press release have been negotiated as part of the contract, the announcement is determined completely by the large company. As mentioned in the previous chapter, it may not even want to mention the name of the smaller partner. If, however, specifics related to the press release have been put into the contract, those in marketing on the smaller-company side now need to do some arm-twisting to ensure that everything is done according the terms negotiated.

Product integration and delivery: Over a period of six to nine months, this is the process that takes the product from integration to delivery. Most likely, the large company has a defined customer rollout process that sets forth what happens step by step. Elements in this process include:

- Initial functional and system analysis

- Initial product planning to create detailed product specs that define in detail the product features and functionality, work flow, and user experience

- Initial testing to make sure there are no bugs or issues in the existing technology

- Initial code drop

- Various cycles of system integration and system testing on both sides: refining, approving, working out bugs, looking for problems, testing, and giving feedback as part of overall quality assurance

- Majority of code now dropped in; more testing and fine-tuning leads up to the first customer beta release

Product launch: The launch is a hard date when the product is available to all customers (a date usually stated in the contract). Ahead of this date, the large company may have negotiated an early delivery deadline as part of a sales agreement with a strategic early adopter customer or with early beta customers.

Marketing, Sales, Training, and Sales Support

Those in marketing and sales at the smaller company can face a steep learning curve. The product manager or chief technology officer may be brought into the product and project planning meetings in order to articulate the product vision, market positioning, and descriptions of key features and benefits. The new market offering might be tested with top salespeople and early-adopter customers to validate the offering. If the large company expects to close a deal with a strategic customer ahead of the launch, there is added pressure to have sales collateral and messaging ready on time.

In the support and operations area, both companies work to integrate the support offerings for customers and partners alike. Onc of the first orders of business for both sides is to determine a common definition of Tiers 1, 2, and 3 support. Once this is done, processes and metrics can be set for support service response times.

A senior technical support person at the smaller company typically assembles a team to provide training for support services.

Technical or engineering staff have the deepest knowledge as to how the two products interact with each other, and therefore need to be available to suggest the kinds of questions most likely to be asked during a support request. There could be participation in each other's training programs to develop a common vocabulary and product development standards.

Negotiating Back Deliverables

When the contract was negotiated, a lot of promises were put down in black-and-white that pushed schedules down to the wire. At the time, the project team at the smaller company may even have stated how uncomfortable they were with the deadlines.

Ideally, those on both sides now assigned to make things happen accept that it may not be realistic to try to make good on all these promises. One partner or both understand that things are going to take longer than originally projected. Perhaps something can be scaled back or adjusted. Negotiating back deliverables gives both sides the confidence that they can complete what has been promised without losing face or incurring additional expenses. For example, instead of a complete demo, perhaps a partial demo will do; or a mutual agreement can be reached to pare back the feature set in the first version.

Revisiting Unrealistic Budgets

Leaders can be notorious for being aggressive, optimistic, and shoot-for-the-moon types when it comes to forecasting sales and estimating delivery times and calculating the required resources. But, at the operational level, crunching code, testing, and revising take time even in the best of circumstances. Early into the integration, it is quite normal for the vice president of engineering or a project manager to request additional budget for more staff as the project deadlines loom closer. They will continue to push back even when told there's no money for a full complement of staff.

They are in a position to do so because now that the integration is under way, developers are able to actually calculate the number of hours it is going to take to write the required code. By showing project leaders the numbers, they can prove that the deadlines are very difficult, if not impossible, to meet with the resources available.

When this happens, it is really hard to fight the math. Regardless of the vision that was set, reality now forces some recalculation of the project expenses and revenue.

"BY SETTING THE SALES GOAL AFTER THE SALES, WE'RE ABLE TO CONSISTENTLY MAINTAIN AN ABOVE AVERAGE SALES QUOTA."

Dealing with Partner Letdown

Although everyone was thrilled to finally be partnered with a large high-status company, it is hard to be successful if the larger company's product isn't stable or developed to the point where it is going to be successful.

For example, it is going to be difficult for the smaller company to deliver if the large company's developer kits aren't ready or aren't documented properly. There could be software defects (bugs), or systems could have been set up in an overly complex manner. These are all issues that must be fixed before moving ahead. Compounding the frustration, such delays tend to happen at a time when developers at the smaller company are being pressured to do more without enough resources, and when the product managers at the larger company are under a crunch to meet the launch deadline.

This is another case where some renegotiation of deliverables may be required, as well as some damage control done on both sides, particularly if launch deadlines are going to be missed. Ideally, the business development person gathers specifics from those working in the technical areas on what is needed to get the project back on track, and then meets with their counterparts at the large company to get agreement on a modified plan.

Politics, Bureaucracies, and Culture Fit

Frustrations like these need to be acknowledged by leaders at both companies, because they spread negative energy at a time when everyone is being pushed to the limit. Although doing so is difficult, it is worth taking time to raise any issues that are getting in the way of a positive work environment.

The sudden change in company direction highlights what happens when two cultures suddenly merge, or rather "collide." Differences in authority and reporting styles become noticeable at this stage in the new alliance. Decision-making in particular can vary widely, with questions being raised such as who is involved in these decisions, how quickly they are made, and how much reporting is expected.

Culture fit is particularly apparent when companies come from different regions or countries. For most Canadian companies, for example, a strategic partnership deal that connects them with a large U.S. company means working closely with counterparts where there can be marked differences in terms of work ethic and intensity, language, communication style, and level of formality.

In addition, the complex bureaucracy can mean endless meetings and processes, which create a drain on resources and time. Those in the trenches are totally absorbed day-to-day with the challenge of moving the project ahead. The last thing they need is another conference call.

For smaller startups, this transition can be particularly challenging. You most likely originally signed up to work with like-minded entrepreneurs where you could walk across the office and talk with each other, face to face. Now your staff counterparts could be located across continents, perhaps even speak different languages. The large company will have its own unique terminology as well as extensive documentation and bureaucracy. Even figuring out how departments connect within that corporation and which ones function together takes time.

The political environment at a large company can be another eye-opener for the team at the smaller company. Before the deal was signed, you probably only dealt with a champion from the large company who believed in the value of the partnership and helped push the deal through. You were mostly protected from the naysayers, typically those associated with internal operations who perhaps felt threatened by the deal or had been vocal about calling out the risks.

After the deal is signed, however, you now find your team exposed to the internal politics of a massive organization. There may be strong independent business units that don't believe in the value of the partnership, and that say so. You may find yourself in the middle of nasty arguments and blame-scenarios. All of this can dampen any excitement pretty quickly.

When working toward a product launch, those overseeing the partnership need to monitor culture fit, be aware of the differences, and talk about where adjustments could be made and what simply needs to be accepted as a new way of working together. Project managers need to step in and suggest adjustments as to how the project is managed. Perhaps there is a limit on the time spent in meetings or the number of staff expected to be in attendance.

If culture fit cannot be solved in the early months, that will make the partnership very difficult, if not impossible, to manage in the longer term.

NURTURING OR TOUGH LOVE— WHICH CULTURE WINS?

When Amazon announced it was planning to buy Whole Foods, some immediately raised the question of corporate culture. In fact, one consulting firm even described the acquisition as a "potential clash of worlds."

Under the leadership of workaholic CEO Jeff Bezos, Amazon had a reputation for being a very tough and demanding environment for employees. Even Bezos likes to boast to his people that "This is a culture of working incredibly hard."

Not surprisingly, Amazon employees routinely talk about the hyper-competitive environment that pushes them, with extremely high expectations and a seemingly unforgiving attitude. Although Bezos claims that this stimulates innovation, some former employees have spoken out about how they felt totally burnt out by the harsh culture.

By contrast, with CEO John Mackey at the helm, Whole Foods' employees speak openly about work satisfaction and the care demonstrated by their employer. The high-end grocery chain is known as being particularly nurturing and supportive, so much so that it has been counted as one of America's "Great Places to Work" every year since its inception.

Although the Amazon/Whole Foods partnership may deliver big benefits for both sides, only time will tell how much culture fit (or clash) is going to affect the success of the merger, or even if one culture is destined to yield to the other.[15]

Keeping the Team Engaged

With a product launch set within a year of the new partnership, continued enthusiasm and engagement are critical. Both partners need to remind staff of the long-term, anticipated benefits for signing a partnership agreement in the first place.

Yet, leading up to a launch, the smaller company has to focus on a set of "less lofty" goals. Although the smaller partner would like to think of the new relationship as being that of a "strategic partner," in many ways the relationship resembles that of a customer-client. The message to your team is simple: Hang in there, get product integration done, and launch the product to demonstrate to the large partner that it made the right choice.

You need all resources in double time. So build engagement from the beginning by involving key people in the initial pitching and negotiation. Bring others on board and find ways to keep them excited about working on the integration to make it all happen. Make every success along the way *everyone's* success, whether it be the first announcement inside the company or the first pre-sales demo. Elicit feedback, ask questions, and listen to ideas and advice as you move through the process.

Those in development have pride of ownership. They work hard because they believe in what they are building. They want to create code that is relevant and appreciated by users. The best reward for them is watching what they've created become a usable solution. Let them know that they are part of why the new partnership is going to be a game-changer for the company.

Money Expectations

Within the smaller company, expectations in terms of compensation, revenue, and overall company profits need to be managed both before *and* after a deal is signed. Up until now, those in sales were motivated by commissions, while project managers were usually motivated by bonuses. On the other hand, developers were motivated by the fact that they had created a shippable product that would be a game-changer in the industry.

But once a partnership deal has been signed, all this can change. During the development phase, it expected that for now, at best the smaller company is going to break even or lose money. There are simply no profits, bonuses, or sales commissions to be had. Meanwhile, the developers are working longer and harder to meet launch deadlines without the benefit of added staff.

When employees start to feel less than enthusiastic about the immediate benefits of signing a deal, help keep everyone focused on the long-term picture. This includes touting the benefits of the partnership in terms of future sales and growth. It also means stressing the added value that the smaller company is on its way to becoming stronger, more reputable, and eventually even more attractive. This relates directly to stock options and their potential.

Stock options (or restricted stock units) are usually offered to everyone in the company, including administrative staff. Although stock options can make employees rich overnight, some may be cynical about their value. For them, until the company creates a public market for its stock or is acquired, a stock option only represents the possibility of value. Remind (or inform) employees of potential long-term gain and their share of the success. No one really wants to talk about being acquired or sold, though these realities need to be understood.

The only way to manage expectations around money is through clear communication and education well before a deal is even in the works. As long as it has been made clear from the beginning, no one should be surprised by a change in compensation or feel unfairly treated.

And Now, for the Next Deal...

There is added pressure for getting the product completed on time. The onus is on the smaller company to make it happen, so you will have developed a strong strategic alliance going forward.

As long as work on the integrated product is progressing fairly well, your CEO or your VP of Business Development can be looking within the big company and other product groups for the next opportunity. Your pitch can now include the benefit of being an approved vendor, with a global master agreement and a support mechanism in place. You can only do so, however, if you can leverage the facts that product delivery is on track and you have delivered on your promises.

Then, after months with heads down and participants well-directed to the tasks at hand, your team gets a sign that you are over the first hurdle: The large partner starts talking about plans for the next 12 to 18 months! This could happen after the official launch or even leading up to the launch when everyone is confident that the product is now ready. The intense pressures you faced over the past year have been overcome. The partnership, to date, has been a success! *Congratulations.*

Next, you need to manage the partnership going forward.

CHAPTER 6:

MANAGING A PARTNERSHIP TO SUCCESS

"Bad companies are destroyed by crisis, Good companies survive them, Great companies are improved by them."

–Andy Grove, Former CEO, Intel

At the 2001 GSM World Congress Trade Show in Cannes, France, Microsoft catapulted its strategic partner, a small UK startup, into the spotlight. The unveiling featured Microsoft's color prototype of its new multimedia smartphone by the handset manufacturer Sendo. The z100 would be the first smartphone running Microsoft's Windows Mobile for Smartphones operating system, a version of Windows CE.

The hype and excitement at the Cannes event would not last. The Microsoft Sendo story became a case study of a strategic partnership gone seriously wrong. Over the next year, the launch of the z100 was delayed several times due to what were described as "technical problems." Then, just weeks before the launch date,

Sendo shocked the IT world by ending the partnership unexpectedly. The company claimed that Microsoft did not provide access to source code, which made it impossible for Sendo to tailor the necessary software.

Consequences of the failed partnership went from bad to worse. Following the collapse of the agreement, Sendo defected to Microsoft's archrivals: Nokia and the dominant mobile software company at the time, Symbian.

Sendo then sued Microsoft for fraud, misappropriation of trade secrets, and unfair competition. Microsoft responded to the lawsuit, accusing Sendo of "gross incompetence."

The suit was settled for an undisclosed sum in 2004. Both sides claimed they were pleased with the resolution. Microsoft, however, continued to flourish; but by 2005, it was reported that Sendo, the once-bright light in the cell phone industry, was on the brink of bankruptcy.

Regardless of the hype and optimism present at the initial unveiling of a new product, things never go exactly according to plan. The Sendo-Microsoft story represents a worst-case scenario of what can happen after a strategic partnership is signed and the reality of working together post-launch sets in.

A partnership can be derailed in multiple ways. Shifts are common in business strategy or market conditions. Perhaps one of the companies undergoes a merger or acquisition, or the large company changes its overall product strategy. In many instances, however, the partnership simply fizzles. When there's a second release, the smaller company isn't included, or the larger company gives the business to a competitor.

In a study conducted by The CMO Council, almost half of respondents (330 CEOs around the world) reported failure rates in strategic partnerships of 60 percent or more.[16] A PwC survey conducted in 2014 for the Global Center for Digital Business Transformation puts the percentage at 65 percent.[17]

Reasons given included mismatched objectives, values, and relevant stakeholders; ineffective governance; and the failure of the partnership to be mutually beneficial. Research done to back up the findings pointed to the same factors:

"Strategic partnerships inevitably involve challenges that have to be resolved efficiently to ensure the longevity and success of the alliance, such as isolating proprietary knowledge, processing multiple knowledge flows, creating adaptive governance and operating global virtual teams.

"If these challenges are not tackled, the partnership will more than likely fail, which, as the empirical research shows, happens in more than half of the cases."[18]

Meet Challenges Head On

The above statistics are far from surprising. Ongoing issues and challenges are going to arise, particularly related to IP and managing teams from two very separate organizations with potentially conflicting goals and styles. Negotiations and, ultimately, the partnership contract all need to be done with knowledge on both sides that success or failure now comes down to managing the relationship.

Some factors may be out of your control. Many, however, you can turn around by being prepared for the inevitable challenges that arise—because they *will* arise—and knowing how to respond. As shown repeatedly, when problems are not addressed right away, dissatisfaction festers. Before long, it becomes clear to one or both parties that the partnership has failed to be mutually beneficial.

What follows are a number of things that can happen and suggested ways in which you proactively manage your way through such challenges.

Turn Problems into Opportunities

Early in my career, I was a manager for a technical support department. I spent my time answering calls from people who were dissatisfied or frustrated because something didn't work as expected. No one ever called me, the tech support guy, because he or she was happy. As a result, the overall tone of each day tended to be negative.

But after the company did a customer satisfaction survey, I saw how customer support problems could be translated into opportunities. Our survey showed that customers typically rated their level of satisfaction "four out of five." Only when there was a problem and an opportunity arose to fix it did they change their rating to "five out of five." It was a valuable lesson. It is the chance to fix something when things go wrong that gives you the fives! In most instances, it makes customers feel special and appreciated.

Negative feedback after the product is released is probably the worst event you could face, particularly if your part is deemed to be the blocking factor for getting the product to market. For example, code that is full of bugs can really shake the confidence of the large company, both in your developers and in you as a partner. It feeds the perception of the large company that you are a typical startup or small company with insufficient resources and experience to handle a large, complex project.

A product with immediate negative reviews creates tremendous pressure from the top levels to fix things "or else." As we read in the Microsoft-Sendo case, such severe dissatisfaction can lead to financial threats, and even lawsuits.

The smaller partner needs to be continuously assessing the health of the partnership by setting and monitoring key metrics and by being ready to make early course corrections to resolve small conflicts before they escalate. You can't make bad code "un-happen," but you *can* demonstrate how quickly you can respond to the problem and take action to remedy the situation.

Attention and responsiveness are keys to keeping the relationship on course and preventing smaller issues from turning into "partnership busting" problems. As soon as customer feedback indicates that there may be something unsatisfactory with those first customer shipments, you need to show genuine concern *and* take action. By addressing quality issues early, you can at least make sure that the customers who depend on you truly believe that you've put your best foot forward to proactively manage (and correct) the situation.

Be on the Side of What Works

On occasion the reason for failure may directly point to the large company—not you. In fact, you have put your best developers on the job and deployed all your resources to keep the big guys happy. But at some point, it became clear to your technical people that the product was not going to be successful in the market. At a time when your company should be looking forward to positive returns, you now are wondering how to minimize your losses. Even worse, how do you explain to staff around you that this great opportunity has been messed up by what you previously described as an ideal partner?

When customer feedback is less than stellar, the worst thing you can do is shift blame, even when the fault actually lies with the large company. Your most logical defense, then, is to produce the very best product or component you can. You need to do so even when your developers can see that the larger project may be headed for failure. You also need to do so to protect your future reputation. The quality of your work is important not just for this one partnership but also for other partnership deals you may have in the works.

By standing apart from what went wrong, without finger-pointing, you may be able derive some future benefit from your part of an otherwise "failed" product. In the face of negative reviews, with luck your component part will be held up as the one positive factor.

SURVIVING A FAILED PRODUCT

When Partnerpedia signed a strategic partnership deal with the gigantic Cisco to build an enterprise app store for the new Cius tablet, it looked like our small Vancouver startup was getting a big break. The plan was to integrate our App Store technology with Cisco's hardware—to create a hybrid phone and communication tablet designed to meet the security, collaboration, and videoconferencing needs of businesses.

Unfortunately, testing of the product continued to show problems with functionality. Partnerpedia technicians could see that the large company's product was doomed to failure. But, even though our team could tell that the hardware wasn't ready to go to market, our development team was under tremendous pressure to deliver.

The predictions of our technical team proved to be right. Not long after the Cius was released, one critical IT review read, "Cisco Cius: Death by iPad." Despite the disappointment, Partnerpedia's App Store was a triumph. This helped cement our company's reputation for developing well-designed and well-functioning products, so much so that it caught the interest of other IT giants. And, in 2013, Partnerpedia together with its AppZone software was acquired for an undisclosed sum by BMC Software for the MyIT self-service portal software.[19]

Continually Demonstrate Value

In many deals, internal champions emerge who help the smaller player make their pitch and convince other company leaders of the benefit of the partnership. But, just when you think you've made great progress (or when the partnership is in full-blown project mode), one of those champions is transferred to another division or leaves the company.

The exit of an internal cheerleader can seriously stall further advancement within the large company. It can even threaten an existing partnership. You've forged a relationship of trust between a senior executive who took a shining to your company, and now that person is gone. You have no idea if their replacement wants or needs the same relationship, or even if they are on your side. At worst, they could be advocates for your competitor. You are now left not only without a trusted supporter but also with someone who could be leaking sensitive information directly to your competitors.

The above points to the importance of keeping up a profile within the large company that is wider than a single contact or a smaller business unit. A smaller company, particularly a startup, can never become complacent even if it starts achieving success. Intercompany relationships are a key business asset. Continue to develop such relationships with more than one person, ideally outside the original circle of contacts. Be seen at events, online, and in person. Show up on everyone's LinkedIn page.

Above all, don't forget why you caught the attention of the large company in the first place. You were not selected as a partner solely on the basis of your part of the product. As stated in previous chapters, large companies look for smaller partners so they can benefit from their ability to innovate, be nimble, be agile, and be able to respond quickly. Keep the spark alive! Continue to evolve a visionary product road map as a way to feed in new ideas and solutions that demonstrate your value beyond the first deal.

PLANNING AN EXIT STRATEGY

A year or two into a successful partnership, additional benefits take hold. You have demonstrated your part in the larger partner's success, and ideally you have begun to embed your technology throughout the various departments and business units in the large company. This is critical, particularly if you've set an exit strategy. The more touch points you have made, the stronger your position will be whenever the question of acquisition is raised. All of this makes the big guy more likely to find a way to keep your expertise exclusively to himself.

Strive for Excellence

The possibility always exists that the senior decision makers may change strategic direction. They may decide that the component that you are providing is now core to *their* business, and not context, so why not build it without you? Or they may buy your competitor, making you irrelevant. Such decisions can totally blindside those at the smaller company who once believed they were on the inside track.

Remember the elephant and its tendency to trample smaller players? Large companies look out for their best interests at all costs. A change in company direction is always a possibility. The market is smart and ever-evolving. Your only defense is to fulfill your part of the project extremely well, and, as much as possible, to prove to be so good at what you do that a change is not viewed as an immediate priority. It's hard to predict who the winners are going to be, so be *excellent.* Continue to talk with other potential partners to protect against forces outside your control. Continued persistence usually wins the day.

SURVIVING "PARTNERSHIP BETRAYAL"

Our first major vendor at Crystal Decisions was Borland, a leader at the time in data management systems. To become a good strategic partner, we'd made a massive investment in supporting the Borland partnership, confident that this was the best possible deal we could have made. Our best efforts were focused on creating a successful product—Crystal Reports—but then Borland bought our competitor, and we felt the rug had been pulled out from under us. With our hopes dashed as to what success would ultimately look like, we tried to figure out what had gone wrong.

We had no control over what had been a strategic decision made by our large partner, but at least we had other deals in the works. Perhaps we could have created a bigger profile within the upper ranks of Borland, but only hindsight, as they say, is 20/20. As it turned out, however, we were better off because of Borland's decision. The second vendor we'd signed with—Microsoft—turned out to be the giant that succeeded in the market. Without a doubt, it was this partnership that turned our little startup into a huge success story. We were glad we had backed *two* elephants in this race!

So Where Are All the Sales?

Disillusionment often sets in at the smaller company when sales don't materialize, or at least not as quickly as hoped. You have jumped through various hoops and racked up expenses in order to be certified or meet some other marketing or sales criteria, and now you don't feel that the larger sales force is putting enough effort into selling. Perhaps your product is in the large company's sales book but it's still not promoted because, to the reps, it's basically an unknown product. All of these factors fuel the sense that the sales force simply isn't trying hard enough.

Persistence and some additional sales and marketing support usually help. The large sales force often isn't familiar about the new product or about the value it delivers to customers. They might feel nervous about taking time and effort to sell a potentially risky new product that could jeopardize their customer relationships and cause big headaches. Maybe they had a bad experience with an outside product, which damaged their reputation and cut into their commission earnings.

The large companies set the rules because they have the power to do so. In most instances, you are just one small addition to their account sheets. You have to accept this reality and find ways of building the confidence of the sales force in your product beyond its actually being the "acknowledged" or "recommended" product. Perhaps those overseeing training can add in some additional webinars on the product features. Sometimes it's just a matter of being the "easier" partner to work with, remaining persistent, and working the process.

Ideally, it's only a matter of time before the product gets added to the large company's standard sales presentation. For instance, there is a long-held belief about SAP that says that unless you've landed three referenced deals, no SAP salesperson would present your product, regardless of how highly it was recommended.

When to Renegotiate a Contract

There will be occasions when the contract needs to be renegotiated in terms of deliverables, schedule, additional features, or functionality. Usually this can be done with a simple addendum. If the scope of change is going to create additional expense for the smaller partner, you may want to take this opportunity to request additional compensation. Don't back down without a spirited negotiation, however. This may be a good time to flatter the large company about its skill in initially negotiating the contract. State that its skill in negotiations has left little wiggle room to add anything extra to the contract. Ideally, a robust and constructive conversation like this could help push forward the argument for a cost adjustment.

Communicate, Communicate, Communicate

Open, direct communication and strong, trusted relationships lay the foundation for success. It's much harder to be caught in a surprise down the road after an issue has been called out ahead of time in a direct, unemotional manner.

Set up communication processes that manage expectations for both the business and the technical aspects of the project. Instead of depending on those in business development to manage all aspects of the account, look at the skill set required and then divide the responsibility between both the technical (functional) areas and business development.

- Technical people are in the best position to manage their part of the project, reporting in during weekly calls on what's working, what needs attention, and the like.

- Those responsible for business development at the smaller company should always be available to project managers for candid discussions about what could be festering on either side related to missing deadlines, integration problems, and relationship challenges. They can also set metrics to track progress and hold monthly meetings where both business and technical staff provide a broader picture of what's going on and discuss issues that remain unsolved. These monthly reporting times are also a good forum for reminding those around the table of the mutually beneficial options at stake and the overall commitment of both parties to make the partnership work.

- Business development also manages the account relationship through the executive chain of command. This may mean reaching out to arrange for the CEO at the smaller company to meet their counterpart at the large company to reset expectations, ask questions, find out what they are hearing about the project, get out in front of any grumbling or dissatisfaction, and generally keep up the profile of the smaller company.

Stay Ahead of the Curve

A lot of companies risk failure because they just don't want to think about the "bad" things that could happen. But they *are* going to happen. By definition, companies are full of people, and people make mistakes. In addition to changes in the market and business strategies, there will be bad code and missed deadlines. To think otherwise is unrealistic.

There can be serious disillusionment at the smaller company because of what does, or doesn't, happen post deal-signing, in terms of working relationships and compensation. Similarly, there may be early signs at the large company that not everyone is fully aligned with the original partnership goals.

It's not what happens that matters, but how you respond that makes the difference. As observed by one European manager experienced in transatlantic relationships, "There really is no good system for working out problems except through personal relationships. If you don't establish good rapport with your counterparts, you haven't got a prayer of making it work. Formal structures of decision making don't do anything for you unless you've got the relationship to start with."[20]

Although circumstances beyond your control can change the expectations of a partnership, leaders and teams ranging from the CEO down need to work together to make the partnership succeed. A supportive culture within each company is essential to making sure the partnership is productive and efficient.

The consequences to the smaller company if the partnership is dissolved are huge. There will be expenses, in terms of development, as well as lost opportunity costs because of time spent on the project at hand. In addition to market embarrassment, you have to face employees who've lost confidence and morale in what was supposed to be a major tipping point for the company.

Strategic partnerships work because you've said it's a priority to make them successful. Successful partnerships take constant monitoring, relationship-building, and expectation management. Don't stop looking for opportunities to be stellar. You and your team need to be putting as much as you can into support and response time, all the while looking for opportunities where you can step up to the plate to show you are indispensable to both your own and the large company's growth and success. The rewards can be tremendous—but none of this happens without dedicated effort on everyone's part.

As my dad always likes to tell me, "If it were easy, they wouldn't call it 'work.'"

CHAPTER 7:

LEVERAGING PARTNER ECOSYSTEMS

"In a business ecosystem, companies co-evolve capabilities around a new innovation: They work cooperatively and competitively to support new products, satisfy customer needs, and eventually incorporate the next round of innovations."[21]

–James Moore

For many years, biologists have used the term *ecosystem* to describe a community of organisms interacting in their environment. The relationships between things matter because everything touches everything else: air, water, minerals, soil, and organisms; and they all influence each other, compete, collaborate, share, create, and co-evolve. They are also inevitably subject to external disruptions, and when this happens, they adapt together.[22]

Noticing growing parallels in the economy, in 1993 the business strategist James Moore coined the term *business ecosystem* to include the interconnected world of commerce.[23] Today we continue to use the term "business ecosystem" or "partner ecosystem" to define a set of companies that exchanges products or services either to serve a common goal or to achieve higher-level individual goals. The terms are also often applied to the technology sector and to the growing number of software ecosystems. Partner ecosystems, however, can certainly expand beyond technology, with collaborators in manufacturing, telecommunications, transportation, and retail, to mention only a few.

Synergy and the Value of Increasing Returns

The value of an ecosystem lies in its synergistic nature. Like ecosystems found in nature, a partner ecosystem is a complex network or interconnected system that works together to form something greater than the individual elements (these elements being the various partners and collaborators). Irrespective of individual size or strength, all players share the success or failure of the ecosystem as a whole.

Partner ecosystems, therefore, become increasingly valuable for all members as interactions increase. Each step in a value chain adds worth to the goods and services before delivering them to the next level in the chain. The better the parts work together and the more choices that are provided, the richer the system.

The cloud-based computing company Salesforce is a model for how partner ecosystems make everything better for participants. The astounding Salesforce ecosystem revenue is three to four times bigger than that of Salesforce as a company. This is because organizations that spend money on the company's cloud computing subscriptions also spend on ancillary products and services, ranging from additional cloud subscriptions and professional services to more software applications, hardware, and managed services. In fact, the International Data Corporation (IDC) predicts that by 2020, for every dollar Salesforce makes, the company's ecosystem will make $4.14.[24]

Partnering Within an Ecosystem

Partner ecosystems are an important model for understanding the underlying benefits of strategic partnerships and how they can be leveraged for even greater value. Every company has suppliers, vendors, and other companies that help deliver on their overall offering. Some are full-blown OEM partnerships; others are vendors or alliances formed through various networks and industry connections. A partner ecosystem takes your business strategy to a higher level than the one-on-one relationships created through traditional strategic alliances and channel relationships. Ecosystems open up a diverse and broader range of functions and industries. Participants might range from partners that provide hardware and applications to customer support sourcing, social advertising, and payment solutions. Some alliances are more formal while others are ad hoc.

Ecosystem partners for a smartphone company, for example, might include the hardware, software, development tools, carriers, app stores, testing, and development companies, even companies managing the process by which the data is shared from one device to another. Drill down and you will find countless partners and alliances, such as those that make, sell, and distribute phones, tablets, printers, Bluetooth devices, the cases that fit the phones, glass protectors, tripods, earphones, headsets, and even selfie sticks. Communication consultants also make money by offering seminars on "cell phone etiquette." The phones they sell are made more valuable by the richness, variety, and quality of their ecosystems. As a result, more phones are sold—but so are more of all the other devices, apps, and services.

SORRY, SON...THERE'S NO APP FOR THAT

"THERE'S AN APP FOR THAT"

Apple created one of the most effective ecosystems in the world, and in doing so transformed its business.

When the iPhone first came out in 2007, Apple's CEO, Steve Jobs, wanted to stay true to his original vision: Keep external development parties out, in order to maintain the high level of design and functional integrity of Apple products. But Apple board member Art Levinson, along with SVP of worldwide product marketing Phil Schiller, urged Jobs to change his original vision. They believed that by building an ecosystem of third-party iOS developers, Apple could get ahead of its rival Microsoft in the cell phone space.

Although Jobs initially shut down the discussion, over time he began to see how an ecosystem strategy could achieve market dominance, particularly when the iPhone had a first-entrant advantage.[25] In a move completely opposed to everything Apple had ever stood for, the company provided app development kits to all interested external developers. (To retain some degree of control and to ensure profitability, apps accepted for the store were thoroughly tested, and 30 percent of the developers' revenues had to be paid back to Apple.)

Apple's ecosystem of external developers ended up creating a huge selling point for the iPhone, iPod Touch, iPad, and Mini. This was a major change in Apple's partnership strategy that had a dramatic effect on the company's business fortunes. Apple's mobile devices became more valuable to customers because of the added usefulness of third-party apps. As a result, smartphone competitors like Nokia and Blackberry soon became almost extinct.

After its initial launch in 2007, Apple would sell more than *one billion* iPhones worldwide. By the first quarter of 2017, iPhone sales accounted for more than 69 percent of Apple's total revenue. Although the Android platform eventually caught up,[26] consumers continue to place more confidence in the apps available through Apple App Store. Steve Jobs's brand promises of quality design and functional integrity live on in the most valuable company on the planet.

Plugging into an Existing Ecosystem

Large companies like Apple, Amazon, Google, Netflix, and SAP have obvious advantages in terms of ecosystems. There is a pent-up demand for leveraging the value of these global brands and their massive install bases from companies both large and small. (We could assume that external developers were salivating for the day when Steve Jobs opened up Apple's iOS to app creation.) However, partner ecosystems are no longer solely for the large companies. Part of a business strategy for smaller companies needs to include an analysis of how you too might benefit from partner ecosystems. Most likely, this means plugging into an existing ecosystem. The starting point is to look at the bigger fish—that is, the large technology vendors and the ecosystems they have created around them. The SAP ecosystem offers a good example.

- The SAP ecosystem is the largest business software ecosystem in the world, composed of both "official" and less-formalized partnerships. SAP's official partners include more than 15,000 SAP partner companies, which account for 30 percent of SAP's overall business. At least half of the company's major enterprise deals, and 85 percent of its new customers, are influenced by these partners.

- Beyond official SAP partners, there are untold thousands of unofficial partners in the SAP ecosystem. These include some two million SAP community network members as well as millions of SAP consultants (more than 200,000 of whom are working at the top consulting partners around the world).[27]

SAP ECOSYSTEM

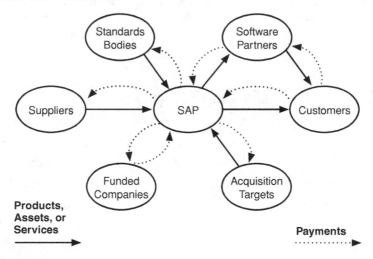

The SAP Ecosystem

For example, if you were looking to participate in the enormous SAP ecosystem, you would have a wide choice of potential partnership and alliance opportunities. Perhaps your company has engineers or technicians who can do integration, or the company could be a solution provider that needs to get its product integration certified. Maybe your company could sign on to one of SAP's partner marketing programs. Or, if you are a training or consulting company, your employees could become SAP certified consultants.

Referring to the SAP example above, there are countless "unofficial" or more on-the-fly ways to tap into other large ecosystems. For example, a company such as yours that builds platform products knows that to be successful it needs to cultivate an ecosystem of developers, partners, system integrators, and other collaborators. Through research, it should identify which providers have the most influence. It should then ask how it might leverage these ecosystems in order to gain a piece of the value being delivered.

If you have a team of application developers with ideas and skills for building apps, you may want to research which large vendors provide developer kits and tools designed for innovative collaborators. The large vendors may also give guidance on areas where they are seeking partner innovation.

LOOKING FOR AN ECOSYSTEM? SEEKING A GAP YOU CAN FILL? QUESTIONS TO CONSIDER:

- Which partners might you collaborate with to make your product more functional to customers? More complete? More convenient to buy?

- Does your competitor have a product or a feature in its product that you could neutralize by adding a "partner product" to your platform or offering?

- Are there areas of innovation that would enable you to leapfrog ahead of your current growth map?

- Is there a partner you could add that would make your product a valued vertical solution?

- Are there implementation partners that could extend and accelerate your ability to grow in the market because your own professional services team isn't yet at capacity?

- Are there service partners who are industry experts that could help you become more useful and valuable to your customers?

Formalizing and Nurturing an Ecosystem

Giants such as SAP and Salesforce have no problem attracting participation in their ecosystems because of their huge customer base. For smaller and midsize companies, it can be more difficult. Once you've identified what you'd like the ecosystem to do for your company, you need to figure out how you are going to demonstrate "what's in it for me" in order to get outside collaborators excited about what you are doing.

The first step is to create a formalized way to participate. You may, for example, create a developer program that application developers can easily access in order to build on top of your company platform.

You will then want to support the program and nurture the external collaborators by making your company easy to deal with, using the following strategies:

- If you are providing developer kits, make them available at low or no cost.

- Provide online tools and training through webinars and certification programs.

- Set up support services for trouble-shooting, and let users know how they can get their questions quickly answered.

- Add sales and marketing support by offering access to special pricing, promotional mailings, and social media campaigns.

- Consider featuring special promotional offers such as "vendor of the month" profiles on your company website.

When I was leading the SAP developer program ecosystem, I would often remind my team that the developers we were recruiting had a choice: They could choose to join our ecosystem and build their applications on SAP, or choose a competitor such as Oracle or IBM. It meant that we had to constantly ask ourselves, "What can *we* do to sweeten the deal so they are motivated to put their best people and resources on developing solutions for our platform?"

Setting Up Your Own Ecosystem

Preparing a manual for creating your own ecosystem is beyond the scope of this book. But it would be worthwhile to look at how you might collaborate beyond one-on-one partnerships. A common mistake that many businesses make is limiting themselves to a few options instead of taking advantage of the entire ecosystem of possibilities. Your underlying product or service will become more valuable if there's recognition that there's an ecosystem around it.

Once you look beyond these traditional partners, there can be multiple ways in which you could connect with others in order to achieve something of greater value. As a smaller, more innovative company, you may find that you are exactly what the big guys are looking for to add value to their ecosystems.

Consider the apps that airlines now offer that make it possible to check in on-line, receive travel alerts, access airport maps, and even order a car through Uber or Lyft as soon as you land. They built an ecosystem of partners to improve the experience for travelers wanting a more convenient way to get through an airport quickly and reach their destination with greater ease and less hassle.

You may not be able to create a full-blown ecosystem, but you *can* identify which kinds of businesses are relevant to you and who the players are.

Are there steps you could take to foster relationships and growth with a wider, value-adding ecosystem of partners and collaborative organizations? Start with only a few partners, making the case with each one for aligning in some way in order to create more value for your end user.

Once again, use *core* and *context* to think strategically.

As an entrepreneurial company, however, you can't do it all, even though you may be used to working that way. Using your understanding of core and context activities, as explained in chapter 1, identify which collaborators you might need in your ecosystem to do "context activities" and which features and functions might be best to leave as "core." Companies have traditionally outsourced context activities when resources are stretched, but sometimes it's not so simple as merely outsourcing context and never letting go of core. If you take on too much core at the beginning of a project, however, you could risk a delay in getting a product out in time—and be beaten by a competitor.

A reminder: Core activities ideally are those tasks that you feel are your "family jewels": These are the ones you want to keep doing in-house. In fact, if you cannot do these activities, then your company cannot survive. Context activities are everything else you need to do to stay in business: These might be tasks such as accounting, delivery, fulfillment, sales training, and so forth.

Making Minimum Viable Product Work for You

Gone are the days when product development stretched out leisurely over 18 months or more. In today's rapidly evolving marketplace, no one has that kind of time, or all the answers. Even customers don't know what they want until they actually buy and use a product. Customer feedback, therefore, becomes part of a more iterative development process.

"So, as you can see, customer satisfaction is up considerably since phasing out the complaint forms."

This new reality has given rise to the term *minimum viable product* (MVP), popularized by an academic and entrepreneur, Steve Blank, and one of his students, Eric Ries. In his book *The Lean Startup: How Today's Entrepreneurs Use Continuous Innovation to Create Radically Successful Businesses,* Ries describes what he calls a build–measure–learn feedback loop for creating new products. The first step is figuring out the problem that needs to be solved, and then developing a minimum viable product (MVP). The acronym means having just enough features to satisfy early customers so that the developers can gain invaluable early feedback for the next release. As soon as you have a product ready "enough," you need to get it out there as a first release.

SPOTIFY MEETS MVP

A good example is the case of Spotify, which chose elements from both the Lean Startup concept and MVP in order to first build their product and then, within six months of launching in October 2008, to grow their subscribers to over one million.[28]

Spotify assumed that there was a market for online streamed music that was legal and could be listened to without any delay in buffering. It therefore employed a four-stage iterative product cycle (Think It, Build It, Ship It, Tweak It) to test its hypothesis and iterate according to user feedback.

For the initial "Think It" phase, developers created a prototype using songs they had on their laptops. Spotify then asked its own employees to try out the product and send it to their family members and friends to try. Once testing with this early working model validated its early hypotheses, Spotify moved through the next three stages. Today Spotify offers millions of songs; as of January 2018, some 70 million paying subscribers worldwide—and growing—use the music streaming service.[29]

Ecosystems can provide an ideal forum for executing on an MVP strategy. By using someone else's ecosystem, a company can test a product at an early stage of development, make adjustments for the next iteration, and, through feedback, continue to innovate. Gathering insight at a "minimal value" level is less expensive than developing a full product—and far less risky. Most important, you are able to put your product on the market before someone else does, and you'll know that it is a product that consumers actually want.

Ecosystems and the Cloud

The cloud has made it much easier for ecosystems to interact with each other. Unlike an on-premise software environment, the cloud means there are fewer barriers to gaining access to a system, developer tools, or applications. Looking at ways of participating in ecosystems dependent on the cloud can be another lucrative partnership opportunity for companies of all sizes.

A leading player in this space is Salesforce.com. From the beginning, Salesforce took a very aggressive pro-partner approach. The giant CRM platform provider skipped the on-premise, client-server model and created an enterprise ecosystem entirely on its cloud-based CRM app development platform, called Force.com, and its app store, AppExchange.

Salesforce stands as an ideal example of the dynamic nature of ecosystems and how a company can continue to create and exchange greater value for the participants. Startups and companies like American Express that choose to participate in the Salesforce cloud-offering derive tremendous value from its ever-expanding and ever-evolving ecosystem.

In a 2016 IDC study, Salesforce partners were polled on what drives them to participate in Salesforce's partner program. The average partner respondent reported an annual revenue growth of 38 percent since joining, and for the next three years it expected annual revenue growth of 45 percent.

In addition, Salesforce and its ecosystem of customers and partners predict the creation of 1.9 million jobs globally from the use of cloud computing, up through the end of 2020. Over the same period, Salesforce customers will add some $389 billion in net-new business revenue, or GDP impact, to their local economies.[30]

"It was much nicer before people started storing all their personal information in the cloud."

The chance to double revenue over the next five years is not the only benefit for partners. A total of 75 partners polled for this study reported other significant benefits from working with Salesforce:

- App Cloud development tools cut the Salesforce partners' development time by 31 percent, compared with traditional development methods.

- App Cloud allowed Salesforce partners to cut the cost of quality assurance by 34 percent and decreased time to market by 32 percent.

- AppExchange enabled Salesforce partners to improve sales-closing rates by 15 percent.

ECOSYSTEMS BEYOND THE I.T. INDUSTRY

The idea of a partner ecosystem has even taken root beyond the technology sector. Retail stores around the globe are opening up their data to external developers to create enhanced customer experiences for both online and in-store shoppers. Target's app, for example, includes a store locator, a barcode scanner to get product details or add products to a list, and coupons for weekly and daily deals. Similarly, with the Best Buy app, customers can scan QR barcodes in the store and read reviews, or compare product specs and track past purchases.

Car manufacturing giants such as General Motors and Ford have done the same with apps for their vehicles. Cars have become like smartphones, in certain respects, because of the growing ecosystem of external developer-partners that are building apps to improve the in-car experience.

Similar to the way Apple turned to outside app developers, both GM and Ford "nurture" outside collaborators to encourage them to add value to their respective ecosystems. Ford's AppLink, for instance, provides developers with Android and iOS software development kits in order to make AppLink-enabled apps available to customers through the Ford App catalog. These apps make it possible for Ford owners to use voice commands for tasks such as playing favorite songs and accessing popular iPhone apps. In early 2017 GM responded with its own "infotainment apps." Interested developers can access a software development kit (SDK) through an online portal provided by GM in order to design, test, and deliver relevant, customizable, and integrated automotive apps for end users.

There Is Always an Ecosystem

Ecosystems are designed to respond quickly to the market in an economy in which the parties involved adapt and change as needed. Because alliances are often less formal than traditional contracts and agreements, there are no guarantees or "exclusives." This is actually one of their greatest values. It is easier to shift directions when you want to take more core work back in-house, find more white space to fill a gap with a different product, or add a new collaborator to your network.

It's all about new ways of adding or creating value. Whichever way, or combination of ways, you choose to interact with various ecosystems (or even to create your own), the same tactics apply in terms of your overall business priorities: Identify your goals, assess where your technology best fits, ask how you can give your product a competitive advantage over another, determine where the sources of future value are, and learn how you might best capture opportunities.

In sum, today's most valuable partnerships are built around creating great user experiences. Ecosystems provide a way of delivering solutions that continually ask questions of and respond to the market around them. By doing so, such solutions become increasingly valuable for everyone in the network. By looking at strategic partnering in terms of an ecosystem, you'll increase the likelihood that your product will be more useful to customers and therefore richer, more competitive, more valuable, and more successful.

> *"For us, it's about innovation, making the best product, and making the ecosystem better and better. If we do that well, more people will switch from Android to iOS."*
>
> –Tim Cook, CEO, Apple, talking about expanding into the India market[31]

AN ECOSYSTEM'S NETWORK OF COLLABORATORS

The following provides a list of the kinds of collaborators in an ecosystem. Where might *you* fit in? How might *you* leverage one or more to create your own ecosystem?

Sales and Marketing Partners

- Co-Marketing Partners
- Value-Added Resellers
- System Integrators
- White Labelers/OEM Partners
- Managed Services Providers
- Industry-Specific Products and Services Resellers and Distributors
- Retailers

Technology Partners

- Platform Extenders/Third-Party Application Developers
- Implementation Tools Providers
- Strategic Technology Integration Partners
- Specialists in Vertical Integration
- Joint Product Strategy Partners
- Platform Providers
- Major Platform Users
- Technology Licensees

CONCLUSION:

PLAYING THE GAME TO WIN

"The audacity of any dream must be paired with the micromanagement of reality."

–Bill McDermott, CEO, SAP

Pixar Studios grew from a 40-person hardware company into a small computer animation company, and over time became an Academy Award–winning movie studio as well as a subsidiary of The Walt Disney Company. But during its first decade, the fledgling studio struggled to survive while a small team of believers slowly built a technological and creative foundation. Fortunately, Steve Jobs had a vision of what he believed the ailing computer division could become. In 1986 he partnered with Ed Catmull and John Lasseter by investing in the company.

When talking about success, Jobs used the story of Pixar as an example: "Pixar is seen by a lot of folks as an overnight success," he said. "But if you really look closely, most overnight successes took a long time."

The best partnerships can take years to reach maximum potential. Building and sustaining a partnership is an ongoing process, and it takes time. You can't expect all the pieces to fall into place on the first day. What creates a win is your approach and your preparation.

The business relationship you are formalizing at the contract stage is more than just a deal. It forms the basis of how you will mutually work together to achieve big, game-changing business results. Clear communication as well as ample preparation in terms of priorities and expectations are paramount. These attributes will continue to play a key role in the success of the partnership, now that you are ready to actually work together.

You'll need to manage expectations in terms of money and timelines. Acknowledge that as you explored going into a partnership, a lot of big numbers got thrown around. That's okay—this is the kind of enthusiasm that initially helped everyone see what success might look like if the result were a home run. But sometimes success is a solid single or a double, and that too is okay.

So adjust expectations once the two companies actually start working together at an operational level. Continue to remind both sides of the possibilities and the value of producing a result that is positive for both parties. It's not always going to be easy. As one business writer put it, "The romance of the courtship quickly gives way to the day-to-day reality as partners begin to live together.... Now more than just the upper echelons of management must work together to make the partnership succeed."[32]

Ideally, your company will be able to navigate the issues that arise both before and after signing the deal. You will meet the development milestones and see the product launched with great fanfare. Reports from the first customer feedback and analyst tours will be positive for the full product as well as for the component that was provided by your company. Sales will be good and within a year the large company will approach you about the next product release.

You then can be confident that you're part of a mutually beneficial relationship—one that will continue to help both partners grow.

All the while, your business development team has been leveraging the positive feedback in order to expand your footprint within other divisions and product groups at the large company. This, too, helps your bottom line. Having more than one project in the works creates a staggered revenue stream from essentially different customers.

You Can Win at Strategic Partnering

"Companies want to partner with other companies that are part of an ecosystem, not on an island by themselves. The island days are gone."

–Tim Cook, CEO, Apple

Is strategic partnering for everyone? In a broad sense, yes—because it is difficult to think of a company that exists in isolation from any kind of alliance or collaboration. With technology moving faster and faster, it becomes more and more difficult to be a stand-alone island.

In today's marketplace, products don't stand alone—and neither do companies, regardless of their size. Everything being done in business today interacts and interrelates with everything else. There are always other products and additional services adjacent to yours, most likely connected to the buying process, the post-sales process, training, support, and countless other kinds of user experiences. And when all the systems are interconnected, there's an expectation that to make those interconnections happen and accelerate the time to market, there will be a need for partnerships.

Therefore, every leadership team should include strategic partnerships on its regular agenda. Each business plan, therefore, should include a partnership strategy—that is, an element that talks about preparing for or developing strategic partnerships.

Strategic partnerships are not a case of "do we partner or not?" Finding ways of playing with the big guys—the elephant in the room—is the way to win. So leverage this reality, grow it, and drive new business opportunities your way. Achieving a truly great partnership is well worth the effort.

ENDNOTES

1   SME: Any organizations with less than $50 million in annual revenue; midsize: organizations that make more than $50 million but less than $1 billion in annual revenue. Source: American March Business Administration.

2   Khalid Saleh, Customer Acquisition vs. Retention Costs—Statistics and Trends (blog), Invespcro, https://www.invespcro.com/blog/customer-acquisition-retention.

3   Leah Goldman, "Groupon's Billion-Dollar Pivot: The Incredible Story of How Utter Failure Morphed Into Fortunes" (blog), Business Insider, May 2011, http://www.businessinsider.com/groupon-pivot-2011-3.

4   James Bessen, "History Backs Up Tesla's Patent Sharing," Harvard Business Review Online, June 13, 2014, https://hbr.org/2014/06/history-backs-up-teslas-patent-sharing.

5   Jillian D'Onfro, "Mark Zuckerberg: CEOs need to take risks, but shouldn't have to do 'big, crazy things'" (blog), Business Insider, August 2016, http://www.businessinsider.com/facebook-ceo-mark-zuckerberg-on-taking-risks-2016-8.

6   Mathew Sekeres and David Ebner, "Whitecaps invisible owner casts large shadow," Globe and Mail Online, March 2011, updated March 2017, https://www.theglobeandmail.com/sports/soccer/whitecaps-invisible-owner-casts-large-shadow/article573189/.

7   Some 99% of SMEs in the U.S. have fewer than 500 employees; U.S. Census.

8   Samuel Gibbs, What does Google want with HTC's smartphone business?, The Guardian Online, September 2017, https://www.theguardian.com/technology/2017/sep/21/google-htc-smartphone-business-hardware.

9   From Zero to 10,000 Clients in Two Years Using Channel Partners, The Review Online, http://firstround.com/review/From-Zero-to-10000-clients-in-Two-Years-Using-Channel-Partners/.

10   Alyson Shontell and Anna Mazarakis, Dropbox founder reveals how he built a $10 billion company in his 20s—even though Steve Jobs told him Apple would destroy it (blog), Business Insider, June 2017, http://www.businessinsider.com/dropbox-founder-and-ceo-drew-houston-interview-2017-6.

11   Karine Avagyan and Michelle Perrinjaquet, Strategic Partnerships, https://www.imd.org/research/insightsimd/strategic-partnerships, IMD Insights No. 36.

12   John Chao, Eileen Kelly Rinaudo, and Robert Uhlaner, "Avoiding blind spots in your next joint venture," Online article, McKinsey & Company, January 2014, http://www.mckinsey.com/nsights/corporate_finance/avoiding_blind_spots_in_your_next_joint_venture.

13   David Donner Chait,"5 Secrets to Landing the Perfect Partnership" (blog), Entrepreneur, November 2013, https://www.entrepreneur.com/article/230049.

14   Sandi Lin, "4 Lessons from Becoming a Salesforce ISV Partner" (blog), Skilljar, November 2015, https://blog.skilljar.com/4-lessons-from-becoming-a-salesforce-isv-partner.

15   Abby Jackson, "The thing that makes working for Elon Musk exciting is the same one that makes it maddening" (blog), Business Insider, November 2017, http://www.businessinsider.com/elon-musk-spacex-culture-2017-11.

16   "Grow from the Right Intro," A Report on the Strategic Value of Business Alliances and Compatible Partner Matching, The Chief Marketing Officer (CMO) Council, September 2014, http://www.bpinetwork.org/pdf/studies/Grow-From-The-Right-Intro-Report.pdf.

17   https://www.imd.org/globalassets/publications/insightsimd/docs/36-–strategic-partnerships-final-20.05.14.pdf http://www.pwc.com/us/en/ceo-survey-us/2014/assets/2014-us-ceo-survey.pdf. As referenced in: James

E. Henderson, Professor Charles Dhanaraj, and Karine Avagyan, with Michelle Perrinjaquet, "Strategic Partnerships," Insights@IMD, 2014, https://www.imd.org/research/insightsimd/strategic-partnerships.

18 James E. Henderson, Professor Charles Dhanaraj, and Karine Avagyan, with Michelle Perrinjaquet, "Strategic Partnerships," Insights@IMD, 2014, https://www.imd.org/research/insightsimd/strategic-partnerships/.

19 "App Store Maker Partnerpedia Acquired by BMC Software," BC Business Online, August 2013, https://www.bcbusiness.ca/app-store-maker-partnerpedia-acquired-by-bmc-software.

20 Rosabeth Moss Kanter, "Collaborative Advantage: The Art of Alliances," Harvard Business Review Online, July/August 1994, https://hbr.org/1994/07/collaborative-advantage-the-art-of-alliances.

21 James F. Moore, "Predators and prey: A new ecology of competition," Harvard Business Review Online, May 1993, https://hbr.org/1993/05/predators-and-prey-a-new-ecology-of-competition/ar/1, accessed March 17, 2015.

22 Danone, "Arthur Tansley: The founding father of ecology was an 'honnête homme,'" Down to Earth Danone Online, August 14, 2012, http://downtoearth.danone.com/2012/08/14/arthur-tansley-the-founding-father-of-ecology-was-an-honnete-homme.

23 Mapping Business Ecosystems, Partnering Resources, 2018, https://partneringresources.com/wp-content/uploads/Tool-Ecosystem-Mapping-Short-Format.pdf.

24 Tyler Prince, "Salesforce Economy to Create 3.3 Million New Jobs by 2022" (Salesforce blog), October 2017, http://www.salesforce.com/assets/pdf/misc/IDC-salesforce-economy-study-2016.pdf.

25 Stuart Dredge, "Steve Jobs resisted third-party apps on iPhone, biography reveals," The Guardian Online, October 2011, https://www.theguardian.com/technology/appsblog/2011/oct/24/steve-jobs-apps-iphone.

26 Statistica, the Statics Portal, 2017, https://www.statista.com/statistics/276623/number-of-apps-available-in-leading-app-stores.

27 Ralf Meyer, "Profit from the SAP Ecosystem—An Overview," E-3 Magazine International Online, November 2017, https://e3zine.com/2017/11/23/profit-sap-ecosystem-overview/.

28 "Spotify reaches one million users," Spotify News Online, March 2009, https://news.spotify.com/us/2009/03/02/spotify-reaches-one-million-users-worldwide/.

29 Chris Bank, "Building Minimum Viable Products at Spotify," Specky Boy Online, September 2014, https://speckyboy.com/building-minimum-viable-products-spotify/.

30 Tyler Prince, "Salesforce Economy," ibid., http://www.salesforce.com/assets/pdf/misc/IDC-salesforce-economy-study-2016.pdf.

31 Thomas K. Thomas, "I'm very bullish on India because of its people, culture and the leadership: Apple's Tim Cook," The Hindu Business Line (online press release), August 8, 2017, https://tinyurl.com/yc3dmozr.

32 Rosabeth Moss Kanter, "Collaborative Advantage: The Art of Alliances," Harvard Business Review Online, July/August 1994, https://hbr.org/1994/07/collaborative-advantage-the-art-of-alliances.

GLOSSARY OF TERMS

Channel partners/Distribution partners: A company that provides services or sells products on behalf of a software, hardware, networking, or cloud services vendor. Systems integrators, managed service providers, original equipment manufacturers, distributors, and independent software vendors may all be called channel partners.

Ecosystem: A synergistic network of partners, third-party vendors, evangelists, and plug-in providers that revolve around a company's or industry's core technologies and product offerings.

Internet of Things (IOT): A network of physical devices, vehicles, home appliances, and other items embedded with electronics, software, sensors, actuators, and network connectivity—all of which enable these objects to connect and exchange data.

ISV (Independent Software Vendor): A company that makes and sells software products that run on one or more computer hardware or operating system platforms. The company may also provide software in the form of virtual appliances that run on virtual machines, or may target the cloud as a vehicle for delivering software.

Joint Venture: A business entity created by two or more parties, generally characterized by shared ownership, shared returns and risks, and joint governance.

Managed Service Providers: Companies that implement a full solution and help their customers manage it, supporting such solutions through various tools and processes.

Medium-Size Business: U.S. enterprises that make from $50 million to $1 billion in annual revenue.

Original Equipment Manufacturer (OEM): A company that produces parts and equipment that may be marketed by another manufacturer. OEMs resell another company's product either under their own name and branding, or as a "white label" product.

SME (Small Business Enterprises): U.S. organizations with less than $50 million in annual revenue.

Strategic Partnership: An agreement between two distinct business entities to share expertise, resources, or competencies for their mutual benefit. Typically, one company seeks out a strategic partnership to fill a gap in its own strengths or to create a synergy that increases its revenue and profit potential.

System Integrators: Enterprise consulting firms that stitch together multiple systems, hardware, and software in order to enable industry-specific, end-to-end business processes (examples are Accenture and PwC).

VAR, or Value-Added Reseller: Part of the indirect sales channel: a company that resells software, hardware, and networking products and that provides value beyond order fulfillment. That enhanced value can take a number of forms. Traditionally, a VAR creates an application for a particular hardware platform and sells the combination in a "bundle" as a turnkey solution. In many cases, such bundles target the applications of a specific vertical industry.

INDEX

expectations
  managing, 106
  money expectations, 69–70
  setting realistic expectations,
    42–43

F

failed partnerships
  Microsoft and Sendo, 73–74
  reasons for, 74–75
  See also challenges to
    partnerships
failed products, surviving, 78
fees, 52
filling gaps, 11–12, 22, 93
Fisher, Roger, 33
Force.com, 98
Ford, AppLink, 100

G

gaps, filling, 11–12, 22, 93
General Motors, 100
Getting to Yes (Fisher and Ury), 33
Global Center for Digital Business
  Transformation, 74
goals of partnering, 7–9
  prioritizing value and goals,
    55–56
Google, 8–9
  acquiring HTC, 22
  acquiring YouTube, 13
  partnering with Uber, 41
Google alerts, using to identify
  contacts, 34
Groupon, 13
Grove, Andy, 73

H

hierarchy of partnering value, 4
Houston, Drew, 33–34
HTC, 22

I

IBM, and Apple, 1
indemnification, 50–51, 55
independent software vendors
  (ISV), OEM partnerships with, 2
innovation, 23
Instagram, 11
Intel, 8

intellectual property (IP), 46, 53
International Data Corporation
  (IDC), 88

J

Jobs, Steve, 8, 33–34, 90–91, 105

K

Kalanick, Travis, 41
Kerfoot, Greg, 1, 17

L

large companies
  choosing partners for, 21
  going after partnerships with,
    28–30
  partnering with, 14–15
  what large companies need and
    what they're needed for, 25
Lasseter, John, 105
launching
  bringing employees together,
    60–61
  culture fit, 66–68
  dealing with partner letdown,
    65–66
  keeping the team engaged, 69
  launch and event dates, 49
  money expectations, 69–70
  moving on to the next deal,
    70–71
  point persons, 62
  renegotiating deliverables, 64, 66
  revisiting unrealistic budgets,
    64–65
  support and operations, 63–64
  timeline and milestones, 62–63
layering, 27
Lean Startup, The (Ries), 97
Levinson, Art, 90
liability, 50–51, 55
LinkedIn, using to identify contacts,
  34
long-term focus, 16

M

Mackey, John, 68
marketing communications, 49–50,
  54
marketing events, 62

ABOUT THE AUTHOR

Mark Sochan is a high-tech executive, entrepreneur, consultant, and speaker. For over 25 years, he has successfully managed hundreds of strategic partnering initiatives as well as mergers and acquisitions, and has grown revenue for clients such as Cisco, Microsoft, VMware, IBM, SAP, Capgemini, and Accenture, to mention only a few.

Mark's unique gift is his experience on "both sides of the table," with an ability to successfully manage complex partner relationships. He has a passion for partnering and partner ecosystems and has worked with the "big guys" as well as with smaller companies and startups on how to build, fund, run, and sell businesses in the competitive and ever-evolving technology realm.

Early in his career, Mark joined a startup called Crystal Decisions (later acquired by Seagate Technology) and built out an OEM channel of over 150 strategic partners. He moved to Silicon Valley and joined another startup called TopTier Software, and then as VP, Business Development, he successfully created strategic partnerships with large vendors, including SAP, Microsoft, and IBM. This led to the acquisition of the company by SAP in 2001. He continued his career at SAP as a Vice President of Business Development responsible for Business Development, Strategic Partnerships, and Merger and Acquisition activity. He launched the SAP Developer Network (SDN) and grew it from zero to 100,000 developers in the very first year. From there, Mark went on to become CEO of Partnerpedia, an innovative enterprise software company, which was successfully sold to BMC Software, delivering multi-million-dollar payouts for investors.

Today, Mark is an independent consultant and an investor at Partner Accelerators, a technology company based in California, where he consults and speaks on partnership strategies, business development, and positioning for startups. When he has time to enjoy his sunny state, he enjoys flying his Piper Lance and spending time with his three sons. He is also an active musician and plays bass in a number of local cover bands.

CPSIA information can be obtained
at www.ICGtesting.com
Printed in the USA
LVHW081303090519
617252LV00018B/434/P

9 781732 399808